THE ENTERPRISE AI PROJECT PLAYBOOK

How to Govern, Deliver, and Scale AI Projects for Measurable ROI

Richard Syal

The AI Project Playbook: How to Govern, Deliver, and Scale AI Projects for Measurable ROI

ISBN: 978-1-9994899-8-4 (Paperback)

ISBN: 978-1-9994899-9-1 (eBook)

Published by EverydayAIGuide Publishing Toronto, ON, Canada

everydayaiguide.com

Dedicated to Belle and Luna, my loyal furry feline companions whose assistance in this book included sitting on the keyboard, claiming the workspace, and insisting upon breaks at exactly the right moments; but whose greatest gift was their quiet love, constant companionship, and the softness they brought to every long hour.

Introduction

Artificial intelligence has moved from curiosity to pressure.

Across industries, leaders are being told that AI will improve productivity, reduce operating costs, accelerate decision-making, modernize customer experience, and unlock entirely new forms of value. Boards are asking about it. Executives are funding it. vendors are embedding it into platforms. Employees are experimenting with it. Competitors are announcing it. In many organizations, the question is no longer whether AI matters. The question is whether the organization can manage AI well enough to turn promise into measurable results.

That is where the real challenge begins.

Because AI projects do not fail only for technical reasons. They fail because organizations underestimate what it takes to govern them, scope them, fund them, sequence them, evaluate them, operationalize them, and sustain them. They fail because teams confuse demos with delivery, experimentation with execution, and activity with value. They fail because enthusiasm outruns readiness. They fail because leaders approve use cases before defining ownership, controls, data quality expectations, adoption plans, or success measures. They fail because the organization treats AI as a tool implementation when, in reality, it is also a management discipline, an operating model challenge, a governance challenge, and an investment decision.

This book was written for that reality.

Managing AI Projects, How to Govern, Deliver, and Scale AI Projects for Measurable ROI

is not a book about AI hype. It is not a book about speculative futures, inflated claims, or generic innovation language. It is not a book that assumes the hardest part is choosing a model or writing a prompt. And it is not a book that treats AI projects as standard IT projects with a few new technical terms layered on top.

AI projects are different.

They are different because:

- Outputs can be probabilistic rather than deterministic.
- Success depends not only on software configuration, but on data readiness, evaluation design, human oversight, process clarity, change adoption, cost controls, and trust.

- The risks are not limited to delays and budget overruns; they include flawed recommendations, poor decisions at scale, policy failures, reputational damage, compliance exposure, hidden operating costs, and erosion of user confidence.
- Many organizations are trying to govern systems, they do not yet fully understand, while being pressured to move faster than their control structures were designed to allow.

That is why this book takes a different approach.

It starts from a simple premise: **AI value is not created by ambition alone. It is created when organizations can govern, deliver, and scale AI in a way that produces measurable ROI without losing control.**

That means managing AI projects requires more than technical literacy. It requires disciplined business framing, realistic delivery design, sharper risk thinking, stronger stakeholder alignment, and a clearer understanding of what "success" actually means in an AI context. It requires leaders to ask better questions earlier. What problem are we solving?

What decision or workflow is being improved? What level of accuracy, consistency, explainability, and human review is required? What data dependencies exist? What new risks are being introduced? What costs will persist after launch? What evidence will prove the initiative is creating value? And what happens if the system performs well in a pilot but poorly in operational reality?

Too many books in this space answer only part of that problem.

Some explain AI at a high level but do not show how to manage delivery in the enterprise. Some go deep on data science but offer little practical guidance for executives, sponsors, project managers, product owners, or governance leaders. Some focus on use cases and inspiration, but not on funding discipline, operating constraints, adoption risks, or benefit realization. Others treat AI as primarily a technical implementation issue, when many of the hardest failures occur in planning, governance, stakeholder alignment, process readiness, and post-launch accountability. Some define AI in project management narrowly as the use of artificial intelligence technologies to support project planning activities.

This book fills that gap.

It is written for leaders and practitioners who are responsible not just for approving AI, but for delivering it responsibly and making it work in the real world. That includes executives, transformation leaders, project and program managers, product owners, architects, data and platform leaders, operations teams, governance functions, procurement and risk stakeholders, and anyone tasked with turning AI ambition into a managed enterprise outcome.

The enterprise AI project playbook matters because AI cannot be managed by enthusiasm alone.

In this book, an AI project playbook does not mean a rigid formula. It does not mean slowing innovation, avoiding risk, or forcing every initiative into a traditional project template. It means giving leaders, sponsors, project managers, technical teams, and governance bodies a practical way to move from AI ambition to measurable business value.

A real enterprise AI project playbook is disciplined enough to be trusted, structured enough to be governed, practical enough to be delivered, and clear enough to be measured. It ties AI initiatives to business outcomes, not just technical outputs. It identifies risks early rather than rationalizing them late. It helps delivery teams understand what must be true before an AI solution moves from idea to pilot, from pilot to production, and from production to scale. It builds costs, controls, evidence, adoption, and accountability into the project from the beginning instead of patching them in after things go wrong.

It also recognizes that AI project management is not only about getting to launch. In many organizations, launch is the moment the hardest work begins. The real test is whether the AI system continues to perform, remains aligned to policy and business intent, earns user trust, withstands scrutiny, adapts to change, and proves its value over time.

An AI project that launches without clear governance, measurement, and operational ownership is not complete. It is merely exposed.

This book is therefore designed as an enterprise playbook.

It will help you think through AI projects from idea to scale: how to identify the right opportunities, define business value, assess readiness, structure governance, manage risk, build realistic delivery plans, engage stakeholders, control cost, measure outcomes, and create the conditions for sustainable adoption. It will also help you avoid the traps that repeatedly undermine AI initiatives: vague problem statements, weak sponsorship, poor data assumptions, inflated expectations, unclear ownership, unmanaged model risk, missing operational controls, and benefit claims that cannot be proven.

Most importantly, this book is written with measurable ROI in mind.

AI initiatives are competing for limited funding, executive attention, and organizational patience. In that environment, "interesting" is not enough. "Innovative" is not enough. "AI-enabled" is not enough. Leaders need to know where value is likely to come from, what it will cost to pursue, what conditions must be in place, how success will be measured, and when an initiative should be expanded, redesigned, paused, or stopped. That is why this book keeps one question close throughout: **How do we manage AI projects in a way that creates real business value without creating unmanaged risk?**

That is the challenge this book addresses.

The opportunity in AI is real. So is the confusion. So is the waste. So is the pressure to move before foundations are ready. Organizations do not need more hype. They need a clearer playbook. They need a way to move forward with discipline. They need a way to deliver outcomes, not just experiments. They need a way to scale trust alongside capability.

They need to manage AI projects, done right.

Part I — Why AI Projects Need a Different Playbook

Chapter 1

Why Traditional Project Management Is Not Enough for AI

For years, organizations have relied on established project management disciplines to deliver technology change. Those disciplines exist for good reason. They bring order to complexity. They define scope, sequence work, assign accountability, manage dependencies, govern budgets, and create a path from business need to operational outcome. They have helped organizations implement enterprise software, modernize infrastructure, migrate platforms, automate workflows, and coordinate large-scale transformation with discipline and control.

Those foundations still matter.

But when organizations begin managing AI initiatives as though they are simply another software project, another automation effort, or another infrastructure deployment, they quickly encounter something different. The assumptions that make traditional project management effective do not disappear, but they no longer tell the whole story. AI work changes the nature of uncertainty. It changes the meaning of readiness. It changes how performance must be evaluated. It changes how risk emerges. And it changes what leaders must manage from the very beginning if they want to reach measurable value without losing control.

That is why traditional project management is necessary for AI, but not sufficient.

This chapter explains why.

The Hidden Assumption Behind Traditional Delivery

Much of traditional project management rests on an implicit logic: the desired outcome can be defined with enough clarity that delivery becomes a matter of planning, coordination, execution, and control.

In standard software projects, this often holds true. Requirements may be incomplete at first, but the organization generally expects that the system can be designed to behave in specified ways. A workflow should follow defined rules. A field should validate against known logic. A report should display the agreed data. A system integration should pass data according to a known mapping. A server environment should meet performance and availability requirements that can be measured against established thresholds.

Even when complexity is high, the project still operates inside a fundamentally deterministic worldview. If the team understands the requirements, builds correctly, tests thoroughly, and deploys carefully, the system should behave as intended. Defects may occur, but they are deviations from an expected result. The project manager's task is to control scope, schedule, resources, quality, communication, and risk so that the intended result is delivered reliably.

AI projects do not fit neatly inside that model.

Not because project discipline stops mattering, but because the object being delivered is no longer only a deterministic system. It is often a capability whose behavior is influenced by data quality, prompt design, retrieval logic, model behavior, training assumptions, evaluation criteria, usage context, human interpretation, policy boundaries, and changing upstream dependencies. In many cases, the team cannot fully specify in advance exactly how the system will perform in every real-world condition. What the organization is managing is no longer just implementation. It is managed uncertainty.

That is the first break from traditional project thinking.

AI Projects Begin with More Unknowns

In traditional delivery, uncertainty typically decreases as requirements mature and the build progresses. There may be hidden complexities, but the project usually assumes that the target state can be defined clearly enough to drive a stable implementation plan.

In AI, the target state itself may begin as a hypothesis.

The team may know the business problem, but not yet know whether the available data can support the intended outcome. The organization may know it wants better classification, routing, forecasting, summarization, search, decision support, or content generation, but it may not yet know what level of accuracy is realistic, what amount of human review will be required, what edge cases will cause failure, or whether the use case will produce enough value to justify operational cost and governance overhead.

That matters because AI projects often start with a proposition rather than a specification.

The proposition may sound clear: improve service response quality, reduce manual effort, accelerate case triage, surface better recommendations, or support faster decision-making. But unlike conventional software logic, AI performance is not simply built to match a fixed rule set. It must be discovered, tested, shaped, and bounded. The project is not only delivering a system. It is learning what the system can safely and consistently do.

This changes the role of planning.

In traditional projects, planning often assumes that the work breaks down into known tasks leading toward a defined product. In AI, planning must also account for discovery, experimentation, evaluation, iteration, and controlled learning. A delivery plan that treats uncertainty as though it has already been resolved creates false confidence. It gives sponsors a schedule, but not necessarily a viable path.

Data Is Not Just an Input. It Is a Dependency That Can Decide the Fate of the Project

Many software projects depend on data. AI projects are governed by it.

That is an important distinction.

In a standard enterprise implementation, bad data is a serious issue, but the system's basic logic may still function. Workflows can still route. Forms can still render. Approvals can still trigger. Reports may be less reliable, but the core system can remain structurally intact.

In AI, data quality, accessibility, relevance, representativeness, freshness, labeling, and governance often determine whether the project is viable at all.

An AI initiative can have a strong business case, enthusiastic executive support, capable technical talent, and a well-run project structure, yet still fail because the data is fragmented, biased, stale, poorly governed, inaccessible, insufficiently labeled, or disconnected from the operational decision the model is supposed to improve. A generative AI use case may fail not because the model is weak, but because the retrieval layer surfaces incomplete or contradictory information. A classification use case may fail because the historical outcomes used as training examples reflect inconsistent human judgment. A forecasting use case may fail because the source data lacks stability or business context. A copilot may appear useful in demonstrations but degrade in production because the enterprise knowledge base is outdated, duplicative, or missing key exceptions.

Traditional project management often treats data as one workstream among many.

AI projects cannot afford that assumption. Data is not secondary. It is foundational. In many AI efforts, the real project begins when the organization discovers what condition its data is actually in.

This means that AI project management must elevate data readiness much earlier than standard project methods often do. Not as a technical afterthought. Not as a cleanup task during build. But as an early determinant of scope realism, cost realism, timeline realism, and benefit realism.

AI Performance Is Not Binary

Traditional project delivery often revolves around pass-or-fail testing logic. A requirement is met or not met. A workflow executes correctly or does not. A defect exists or does not. Even where there are performance thresholds, the evaluation model remains relatively crisp.

AI does not behave that way.

An AI system can be useful, flawed, impressive, inconsistent, safe in one context, risky in another, and difficult to classify through binary judgment alone. It may perform well on common cases while failing on rare but important ones. It may appear strong in pilot conditions but weaken under production variability. It may provide excellent draft outputs that still require human review. It may improve speed while reducing confidence. It may increase coverage but introduce subtle quality concerns. It may satisfy one stakeholder group while alarming another.

This creates a fundamentally different management challenge.

In AI, performance is often a matter of thresholds, tolerances, and trade-offs rather than absolute compliance. Leaders must decide what level of accuracy is acceptable, what types of error are tolerable, where human oversight must remain in place, when confidence scores matter, what escalation paths are required, and how performance will be judged across different scenarios. The project cannot succeed merely by "working." It must perform well enough, consistently enough, safely enough, and explainable enough for the intended use.

That is a harder management question than it first appears.

Because once performance becomes non-binary, governance becomes more important. Success must be defined with greater care. Evaluation must be designed more deliberately. Business owners must engage more deeply. And project leaders must resist the temptation to treat a promising demo as proof of production readiness.

Experimentation Is Not a Side Activity

In many traditional projects, experimentation may occur at the edges. Teams may prototype an interface, test an integration approach, or evaluate vendor options. But the project is still largely oriented toward executing a known design.

AI projects require experimentation as part of the core delivery model.

Teams often need to test multiple approaches before settling on one that is viable. They may compare prompts, embeddings, retrieval methods, model choices, guardrail strategies, data preparation methods, evaluation frameworks, or human-in-the-loop patterns. They may discover that a use case initially framed as automation is better delivered as decision support. They may find that a seemingly high-value opportunity is too costly, too inaccurate, too risky, or too operationally complex to scale.

This does not mean AI projects are unmanageable. It means they must be managed differently.

When experimentation is real, the project plan must create room for it. Governance must recognize it. Sponsors must understand it. Budgeting must support it. Success criteria must account for it. A delivery model that pretends the right approach is already known often drives one of two outcomes: either the team hides uncertainty until it becomes a problem, or leadership forces premature certainty onto a use case that is not ready for it.

Neither leads to good outcomes.

Good AI project management does not eliminate experimentation. It disciplines it. It defines what is being tested, why it matters, how results will be judged, who decides whether to proceed, and what evidence is required before moving from experiment to operational commitment.

The Technology Beneath the Project Can Change While the Project Is Underway

Traditional software projects usually assume a relatively stable technical foundation during delivery. The application version may be fixed. The infrastructure path may be known. The core platform capabilities may not change significantly during the project window.

AI introduces a more fluid environment.

Models evolve. Vendors update features. APIs change. pricing shifts. New safeguards appear. Existing capabilities improve or degrade. Context windows expand. latency characteristics move. Retrieval architectures mature. Enterprise tooling changes. Regulatory scrutiny increases. Internal policies tighten. What looked like an acceptable design six months ago may no longer be the best path by the time the organization is ready for scale.

This creates two risks at once.

The first is instability. Teams may build on assumptions that no longer hold by the time deployment decisions are made. The second is distraction. Organizations can become trapped in continuous reconsideration, constantly tempted by the next model, the next vendor claim, the next capability release, or the next architectural trend.

Traditional project discipline alone does not resolve this tension.

AI project management must therefore create a structure that is stable enough to deliver and flexible enough to adapt. That means anchoring the initiative to business outcomes, governance principles, evaluation evidence, and operating requirements rather than to vendor excitement or technical novelty alone. It means distinguishing between meaningful changes and noise. It means knowing when to adapt the plan and when to hold the line.

Without that discipline, AI projects are easily pulled off course.

Trust Is Not a Soft Issue. It Is a Delivery Condition

Many traditional projects include change management, communication, training, and stakeholder engagement. These are important in any transformation effort. But with AI, trust becomes more central and more fragile.

Users are not simply being asked to adopt a new interface or follow a new workflow. They are being asked to work with outputs that may be probabilistic, opaque, or context-sensitive. Managers may be asked to rely on recommendations they cannot fully inspect. Frontline teams may be asked to act on classifications, summaries, or suggestions generated by systems that occasionally sound more confident than they deserve. Compliance, legal, and risk stakeholders may be asked to approve use cases whose failure modes are less familiar than those of conventional software.

If trust is weak, adoption becomes superficial. Workarounds appear. Oversight becomes inconsistent. Escalations increase. Skepticism hardens. Executives hesitate to scale. In some cases, a technically functioning solution fails because the organization never developed enough confidence in how it behaves, when it should be used, or where its boundaries lie.

That is why trust is not merely a communications issue. It is an operational condition.

AI project management must account for explainability, transparency, monitoring, governance, user confidence, escalation design, and responsible human oversight from the start. The question is not whether the tool can produce output. The question is whether people can use it responsibly, defend it credibly, and rely on it appropriately.

A project that ignores this will confuse technical deployment with real adoption.

Deployment Is Not the End of the Project

In many organizations, projects are treated as successful once the planned capability is delivered into production. Post-launch support matters, but the primary project objective is often defined around implementation completion.

That mindset is dangerous in AI.

An AI capability may appear successful at launch and still fail over time. Data may drift. user behavior may shift. policies may change. edge cases may accumulate. model performance may degrade in unnoticed ways. Cost patterns may become unsustainable. Human reviewers may lose discipline. New regulatory expectations may emerge. Business stakeholders may discover that the operational burden is heavier than expected. What worked in pilot conditions may no longer work at scale.

For this reason, AI initiatives require a lifecycle view that extends beyond implementation.

Measurement must continue after deployment. Governance must remain active. Retraining, re-evaluation, control tuning, content updating, and oversight patterns may all need to evolve. Benefits must be validated against actual outcomes, not assumed from early enthusiasm. An AI project that ends at launch leaves the organization exposed to performance drift, cost drift, and trust drift.

Traditional project management often hands off into operations. AI demands a tighter relationship between delivery and ongoing operational accountability.

What This Means for the Project Manager, Sponsor, and Enterprise

None of this means that traditional project management should be abandoned. On the contrary, AI projects need strong discipline. They need clear ownership, governance, structure, decision rights, funding control, stakeholder coordination, risk tracking, communication, and execution management. The problem is not that project management is irrelevant. The problem is that standard project management, by itself, does not fully address the nature of AI work.

AI initiatives require a broader management discipline.

That discipline must combine project execution with data realism, evaluation design, governance rigor, experimentation control, trust management, and post-launch accountability. It must recognize that some uncertainty cannot be scheduled away. It must treat business readiness and operational readiness as seriously as technical readiness. It must define success in terms that are meaningful for AI, not borrowed uncritically from traditional software delivery. And it must keep value, control, and measurability in view at the same time.

For the project manager, this means leading more than plan execution. It means managing ambiguity without masking it. It means helping stakeholders understand what is known, what is not yet known, what must be tested, and what evidence is required before confidence is justified.

For the sponsor, it means funding not just build activity, but disciplined learning. It means demanding measurable value while also recognizing the need for staged validation. It means asking harder questions about readiness, risk, adoption, and ongoing ownership before scale is approved.

For the enterprise, it means accepting that AI is not just a technology wave to be installed. It is a capability class that requires stronger judgment, sharper governance, and more mature delivery leadership.

Why AI Product Discovery Is Not the Same as Enterprise AI Delivery — and Why It Matters

Many widely taught AI frameworks begin in the right place. They tell teams to define the problem, form an AI hypothesis, assess the data, test a proof of concept, validate with users, and only then move toward an MVP and scale. That is not flawed thinking. In fact, it is useful discipline. It helps organizations avoid building AI for novelty alone. It pushes teams to connect technical possibility to user value. It reminds leaders that a promising model is not the same as a meaningful solution.

That discipline deserves respect.

But it is still not enough.

A product-discovery framework is built to answer an important but narrow question: **Could this AI capability create value for a user?** Enterprise AI project management must answer a broader and more demanding set of questions: **Can this capability be trusted, governed, funded, integrated, operated, supported, monitored, defended, and scaled in a real organization?**

That difference is not academic. It is where many AI initiatives succeed in concept and fail in practice.

A proof of concept may show that the model performs well in a limited environment. A pilot may show that users like the speed, convenience, or novelty. A hypothesis may be validated strongly enough to justify further investment. Yet as the initiative approaches production, the real enterprise questions begin to emerge. Who owns the risk? What data is allowed, and under what controls? How is privacy protected? What level of error is acceptable? Who makes the final decision when the model is uncertain? How does the solution fit into existing workflows, systems, approvals, and support structures? What evidence exists for audit, compliance, or executive review? What is the cost to run, monitor, retrain, and sustain it over time? What happens when performance degrades, drift appears, or trust breaks?

These questions do not appear after delivery. They shape whether delivery is possible at all.

This is why the distinction matters. A team may prove that an AI feature is useful and still fail to make it viable. The business may like the idea but reject the risk. Users may appreciate the speed but distrust the output. Legal, security, operations, or compliance teams may block rollout because the controls were never built into the design. Finance may support the pilot but question the economics of scaling it. Leaders may celebrate the experiment and still have no defensible path to operational adoption.

In other words, an AI feature can succeed in discovery and still fail in delivery.

That is the gap this book addresses.

Managing AI projects well requires more than experimentation discipline. It requires management discipline across the full enterprise lifecycle: governance, funding, data readiness, architecture, security, human oversight, change management, measurement, operating model design, and scale controls. The challenge is not only to prove that AI can work. The challenge is to prove that it can work under real business conditions, with real accountability, and for measurable ROI.

This matters because organizations do not capture value from AI when a demo works. They capture value when AI can be deployed repeatedly, trusted consistently, governed responsibly, and scaled without creating unmanaged risk or runaway cost. It matters because trust is not created by model accuracy alone. Trust is created when leaders can explain what the system does, where its data comes from, what its limits are, who is accountable for its behavior, and what safeguards exist when it fails. It matters because enterprise AI rarely remains a standalone feature. Once it enters live workflows, it begins to influence decisions, operations, service quality, customer experience, employee experience, and institutional risk.

That is why product discovery and enterprise delivery must be treated as related, but not interchangeable. One helps prove potential. The other determines whether potential becomes durable value.

In enterprise settings, it is not enough to show that AI works. Leaders must show that it works under control.

A New Management Discipline for AI

The central argument of this book begins here: AI projects must be managed through a different lens.

Not because deadlines no longer matter. They do.
Not because budgets no longer matter. They do.
Not because scope, risk, and stakeholder alignment no longer matter. They do.

But because AI adds a layer of uncertainty, dependence, variability, and trust sensitivity that traditional project methods were not designed to handle alone.

That is why AI project management must expand the discipline. It must govern experimentation instead of hiding it. It must test data readiness before overcommitting. It must evaluate usefulness, risk, and consistency rather than assuming binary acceptance criteria will be enough. It must build trust into the deployment model. It must plan for changing technical conditions. And it must treat operational accountability as part of delivery, not as someone else's problem after launch.

This is not a rejection of project management. It is its evolution.

Organizations that fail to make that shift will continue to run AI initiatives with the language of control but without the mechanisms required to earn it. They will confuse activity with progress, pilots with proof, and launch with value. They will approve projects that sound strategically important but are not operationally ready. And they will discover, often too late, that managing AI well requires a more complete discipline than the one they brought forward from traditional delivery.

Organizations that make the shift, however, gain something important. They gain a better way to decide what should move forward, what should be redesigned, what should be governed more tightly, and what should not scale yet. They gain a way to convert AI from organizational pressure into managed value.

That is the work ahead.

And it begins by recognizing a simple truth:

Traditional project management remains essential.
For AI, it is just not enough.

Figure 1 — Enterprise AI Delivery Requires Both Technical Progression and Management Control

Technical AI work often moves through hypothesis, data preparation, feasibility testing, release, and scale. Enterprise AI project management must govern that progression through value framing, readiness checks, delivery controls, and operational oversight.

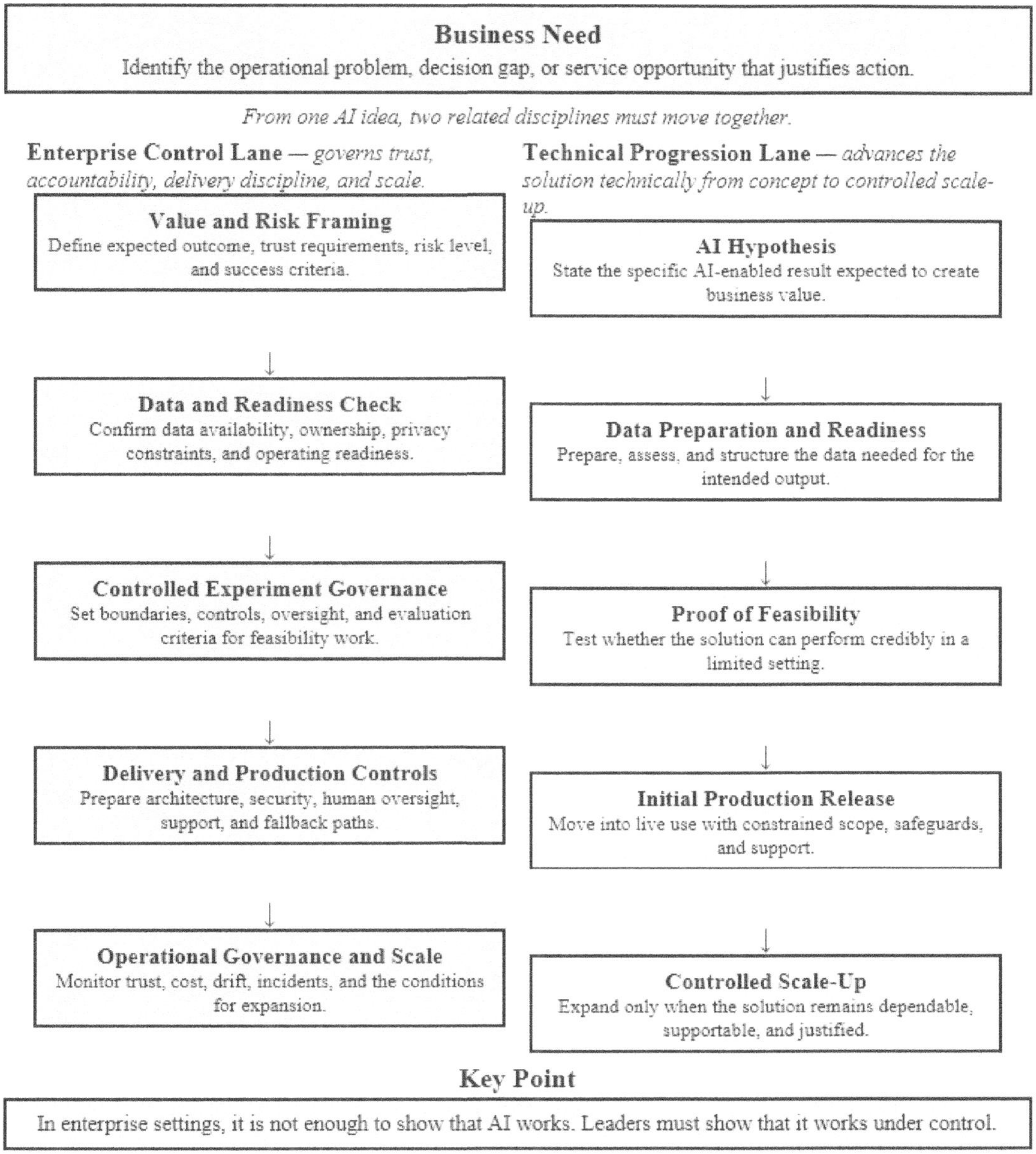

Figure 2 — Traditional vs. AI Project Management

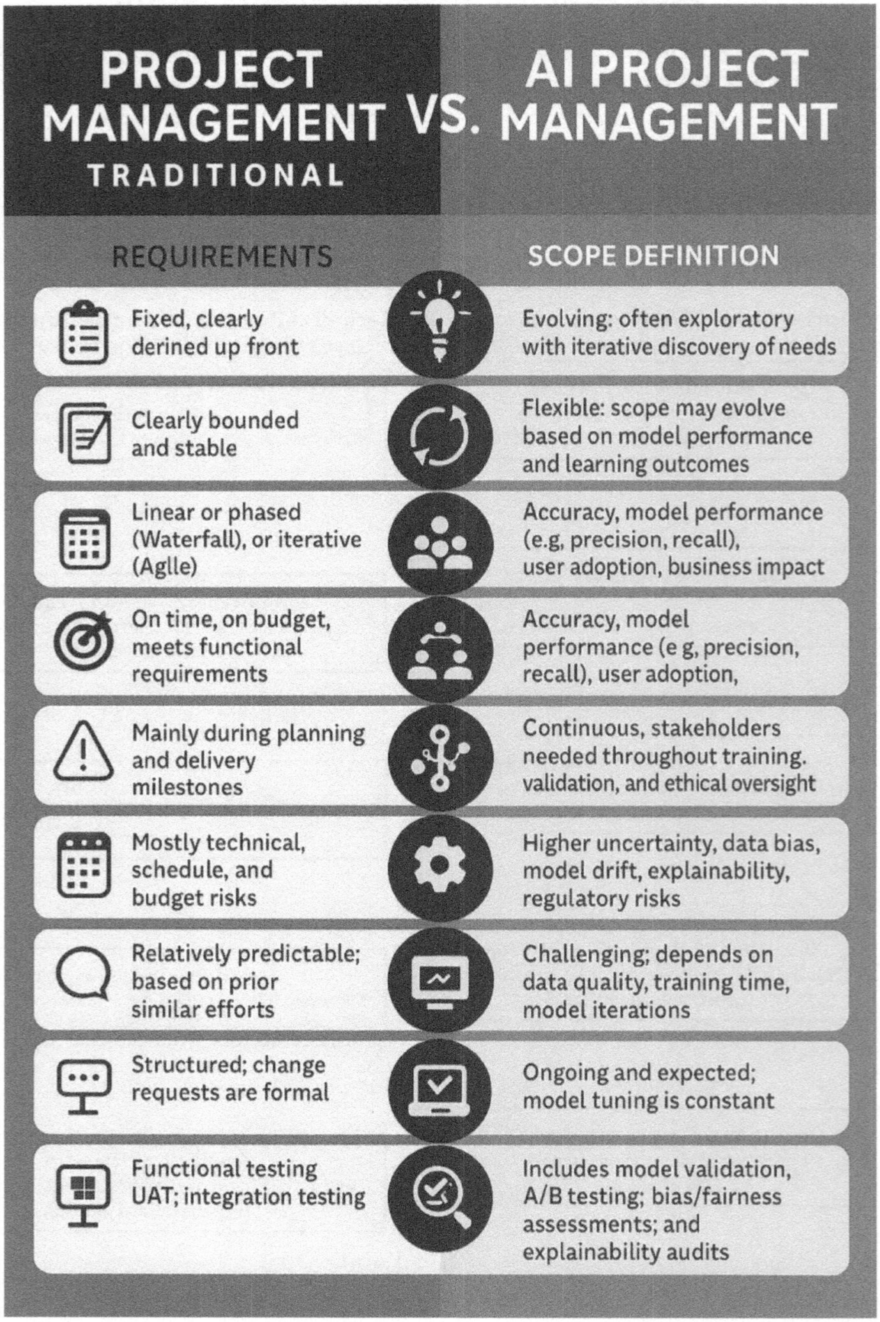

Chapter 2

The Gaps Most AI Project Books Still Leave Behind

By this point, the reader may reasonably ask a fair question:

If AI has become so strategically important, and if organizations are already investing heavily in it, why is there still so much confusion about how to manage AI projects well?

It is not because there are no books on AI.

There are many.

There are books that explain what AI is, how machine learning works, what generative AI can do, how data science teams think, how automation is evolving, how leaders should prepare for disruption, and how businesses can identify promising use cases. There are books that focus on technical design, books that focus on future trends, books that focus on ethical concerns, books that focus on prompting, and books that focus on innovation opportunities. Some are thoughtful. Some are useful. Some are strong within their chosen scope.

And yet, a practical gap remains.

That gap appears the moment an organization tries to move from interest to execution. It appears when leaders must decide which AI initiatives deserve funding, what conditions must be true before launch, how performance should be evaluated, how risk should be governed, how business ownership should be defined, how value should be measured, and how an initiative should be scaled without creating unmanaged cost or exposure. It appears when the question is no longer "What is AI?" or even "What can AI do?" but rather: **How do we manage AI projects in the enterprise so they produce measurable value under real-world constraints?**

Too few books answer that question directly.

That is the gap this book was written to fill.

The Problem Is Not a Lack of AI Content. It Is a Lack of Management Guidance

The AI book market is crowded with explanation, commentary, inspiration, and speculation. That is not surprising. AI is one of the defining technology shifts of this era, and readers naturally want to understand what it means.

But understanding AI conceptually is not the same as managing AI operationally.

A leader may finish a well-written AI strategy book and still not know how to govern a pilot before expansion. A project manager may read an AI overview and still not know how to structure delivery when outcomes are uncertain and evaluation is non-binary. A sponsor may understand the promise of generative AI and still not know how to decide whether a use case is ready for funding. A governance team may absorb general discussions on ethics and still not know what controls must exist before deployment. A business owner may feel convinced that AI matters and still not know how to prove that an initiative is creating measurable ROI rather than producing attractive but weakly governed activity.

This is where many readers are left stranded.

They are told why AI matters. They are shown what AI can do. They are warned that AI introduces risk. But they are not given a sufficiently practical playbook for managing AI initiatives from business case through delivery, control, adoption, measurement, and scale.

That missing layer matters because organizations do not succeed with AI through awareness alone. They succeed when they can convert ambition into managed execution.

Many Books Explain AI. Fewer Explain How to Deliver It

One of the most common gaps in this segment is a strong front-end explanation followed by a weak delivery model.

Some books do an excellent job making AI accessible. They clarify terminology, explain major capability types, describe how models learn, introduce generative AI concepts, and help non-technical leaders become more literate in the field. That is useful. In many organizations, this is still necessary.

But literacy is only the beginning.

Once the initiative enters the delivery phase, the hard questions change. What are the true dependencies? What must be proven before budget is expanded? What business process is being changed? What human review is required? What data deficiencies threaten the use case? What thresholds will define acceptable performance? What governance body owns approval? How should pilots be structured so they generate meaningful evidence rather than superficial optimism? What happens when an AI output is useful but inconsistent? What is the rollback path if trust weakens after launch? How will value be measured beyond anecdotal improvement?

These are project questions. Management questions. Governance questions. Funding questions. Operational questions.

And they are often the least developed part of the AI book landscape.

Many books stop near the point where enterprise difficulty begins. They prepare the reader to understand AI, but not fully to deliver it.

This book is built for that second challenge.

Many Books Focus on Technology. Enterprise Leaders Also Need an Operating Model

Another recurring gap is that AI is often presented primarily as a technology topic.

The technical dimension matters, of course. Architecture matters. Model choice matters. Retrieval design matters. Integration patterns matter. Security matters. Evaluation mechanics matter. None of these are optional.

But enterprise AI does not succeed through technology decisions alone.

It succeeds when the organization has an operating model that can support responsible delivery. That means defined ownership. Clear decision rights. Governance checkpoints. Risk review. Business sponsorship. Funding logic. Benefit tracking. Escalation paths. Post-launch accountability. Change support. Policy boundaries. Human oversight. Auditability. Continuous measurement.

Without that operating model, even technically promising initiatives struggle to scale. The organization may achieve a convincing demo and still be unable to move to production with confidence. It may launch an early capability and then discover that no one clearly owns ongoing performance. It may approve a use case based on perceived innovation value, only to find later that adoption is weak, costs are opaque, and risk ownership is scattered.

This is one reason AI initiatives often stall between experimentation and scale.

The challenge is not merely that the model is imperfect. The challenge is that the enterprise was not prepared to manage the capability as an operational system.

Many books acknowledge the need for responsible AI in principle. Fewer walk the reader through what that responsibility means in terms of actual delivery and operating structure.

This book does.

Many Books Discuss Use Cases. Fewer Show How to Decide Which Ones Deserve to Move Forward

Use cases are one of the most common entry points into AI discussion. Leaders are encouraged to identify opportunities in service, operations, sales, finance, HR, product development, knowledge management, analytics, and decision support. This is often helpful. It gives shape to possibility.

But use case enthusiasm can create its own problem.

Once a list of opportunities exists, organizations still need a discipline for deciding what should be funded, what should be piloted, what should be redesigned, what should be sequenced later, and what should not proceed at all. They need a way to distinguish between visible ideas and viable initiatives.

That is harder than it sounds.

Some use cases are strategically attractive but operationally immature. Some appear easy but depend on poor-quality data. Some promise productivity gains that disappear once human review effort is considered. Some are technically feasible but politically hard to adopt. Some carry limited direct ROI but high trust risk. Some should begin as narrow decision-support capabilities rather than broad automation. Some should not be attempted until surrounding processes are stabilized. Some are better framed as knowledge improvement efforts than AI deployments. Some are too expensive for the value they are likely to generate.

A good AI project book must help readers think this way.

It must move beyond idea generation into decision discipline. It must show how to assess readiness, value, control burden, operational impact, stakeholder risk, and measurement potential before momentum turns into waste.

Too often, that layer is missing.

Readers are given catalogs of possibility when what they need is a framework for choosing responsibly.

Many Books Address Ethics at a High Level. Fewer Translate Ethics into Controls

Ethics is an essential part of the AI conversation. Questions of fairness, bias, transparency, accountability, privacy, explainability, and harm are not theoretical side issues. They are central to whether AI can be trusted, defended, and sustained.

But ethics discussions often remain abstract.

Organizations may finish an ethics-oriented chapter with stronger awareness and still be unsure what that means in practice. What controls are required before a system may generate external-facing content? What oversight must remain in place when recommendations affect people? How should exceptions be reviewed? What evidence should be logged? What policies must exist for human escalation? What does meaningful transparency look like in a business workflow? How should accountability be assigned when output is probabilistic but business action is real? How much explanation is enough for a use case to remain governable?

This is where principle must become management.

A project cannot be governed through ethics language alone. It requires design choices, approval logic, process safeguards, monitoring patterns, response paths, and operational accountability. Ethics matters most when it becomes actionable.

That translation is often underdeveloped.

This book treats governance as something more concrete. Not merely a set of values to affirm, but a set of mechanisms to define, document, apply, and sustain.

Many Books Talk About Innovation. Fewer Stay Close Enough to ROI

There is no shortage of books encouraging organizations to innovate with AI. Some are persuasive. Some are energizing. Some rightly push leaders to think bigger.

But innovation language can drift away from investment discipline.

In enterprise settings, AI initiatives compete against other demands on money, talent, governance bandwidth, and executive focus. In that environment, leaders cannot rely on novelty alone. They must understand where value is expected to come from, how it will be measured, what costs will persist after deployment, what controls must be funded to support trust, and when an initiative should be expanded, paused, redesigned, or stopped.

That requires a more grounded conversation.

A strong AI project book must remain close to business case logic. It must deal with baseline conditions, target outcomes, measurable benefit, implementation cost, operational cost, adoption risk, value leakage, and proof thresholds. It must help readers think clearly about what counts as return, what counts as overhead, what counts as avoidable waste, and what evidence is strong enough to justify scaling.

This is especially important because AI can create the illusion of value before value is proven.

A system may generate elegant outputs and still fail to improve the workflow it was meant to enhance. A pilot may impress executives and still collapse under operational conditions. A use case may save time for one group while imposing hidden review effort on another. A platform may look cost-effective during experimentation and become expensive when volume, monitoring, human review, retraining, support, and governance are included. An initiative may seem successful simply because the organization never defined a hard enough measurement standard.

This book stays close to ROI because enterprise AI must.

It treats value as something to be evidenced, not assumed.

Many Books Are Either Too Technical for Managers or Too General for Delivery Leaders

Another major gap in the segment is audience imbalance.

Some books are written primarily for technical readers. They may be excellent for data scientists, engineers, architects, or deeply technical practitioners, but they do not fully serve the executive sponsor, the program lead, the project manager, the product owner, the transformation office, the governance lead, or the cross-functional leader responsible for turning the initiative into an enterprise outcome.

Other books move too far in the opposite direction. They remain broad, conceptual, and inspirational, but do not give enough structure for actual delivery leadership.

What many organizations need instead is a bridging text.

They need a book that is serious enough for enterprise leaders, practical enough for delivery teams, and structured enough for governance and business stakeholders to use as a shared reference point. They need a playbook that respects technical complexity without requiring every reader to become a specialist. They need a framework that speaks to management decisions, operating risk, delivery structure, and measurable outcomes in a language that business and technology leaders can use together.

That is the intended role of this book.

It is not written as a technical manual for model builders alone. Nor is it written as a high-level executive meditation detached from delivery reality. It is written for the enterprise middle ground where strategy, governance, execution, and accountability must meet.

Many Books Understate the Difficulty of Moving from Pilot to Scale

This may be one of the most important gaps of all.

A great many organizations can launch a pilot.

Far fewer can scale AI well.

The reason is simple: pilots are often protected environments. Data may be curated. user groups may be cooperative. edge cases may be limited. review effort may be tolerated. executive patience may be high. governance scrutiny may be lighter. Volume may be lower. Architectural compromises may be temporarily accepted.

Scale changes everything.

At scale, inconsistency becomes more visible. Drift matters more. Human review becomes more expensive. Exceptions multiply. Policy exposure rises. Auditability matters. Adoption patterns become uneven. Integration dependencies harden. Cost behavior becomes more important. Stakeholder tolerance narrows. Business units ask harder questions. Regulators, auditors, and control functions become more involved. The organization needs clearer evidence, stronger controls, and more durable ownership.

Many books do not spend enough time in that transition zone between promising pilot and sustainable enterprise deployment.

But that is where some of the most expensive mistakes occur.

This book pays particular attention to that transition because it is where management discipline matters most. It helps readers think through what must be true before scale is attempted, how to recognize premature scaling pressure, and how to define operational readiness in a way that is credible, not cosmetic.

Many Books Treat Governance as a Constraint. This Book Treats It as an Enabler of Scale

Governance is sometimes framed as the force that slows innovation down. In weak organizations, it sometimes does. But in serious enterprises, governance is what makes scale defensible.

Without governance, AI may move quickly for a while. It may even appear successful in early phases. But once the stakes rise, the lack of governance becomes the reason the initiative cannot expand. Questions emerge that no one can answer cleanly. Ownership is unclear. Approval logic is informal. Monitoring is insufficient. Risk decisions were never documented. Data rights are uncertain. Human escalation paths are vague. Performance evidence is thin. Cost controls are reactive. Auditability is partial. Confidence weakens.

At that point, governance is no longer a burden being imposed from outside. It is the missing structure that should have been built in from the beginning.

Too many books discuss governance either in overly narrow compliance language or in a broad ethical tone without showing how governance supports execution, trust, and scale.

This book treats governance differently.

Here, governance is part of the delivery model. It is what helps the enterprise know what is safe to pursue, what must be reviewed more carefully, what evidence is required, what controls are proportionate, what ownership must exist, and what conditions must be satisfied before scaling. Good governance does not block value. It protects value from collapsing under unmanaged risk.

What This Book Does Differently

This book was written to address the gaps above in a practical and integrated way.

It does not begin and end with AI explanation. It focuses on how to govern, deliver, and scale AI initiatives in the enterprise.

It does not treat AI as merely a technical problem. It treats AI as a management challenge involving operating model design, stakeholder alignment, investment discipline, trust, risk, and measurable outcomes.

It does not stop at use cases. It helps readers assess which opportunities deserve to move forward and under what conditions.

It does not discuss responsible AI only in principle. It translates responsibility into management structures, control expectations, and delivery decisions.

It does not celebrate innovation without questioning value. It stays close to ROI, cost realism, and benefit proof.

It does not assume one audience. It is designed to serve leaders across business, delivery, governance, and technical functions who need a common playbook.

And it does not confuse pilots with enterprise success. It pays close attention to what happens between ambition and operational scale.

In that sense, this book is deliberately positioned in the space many readers still struggle to find: the space between AI excitement and enterprise execution.

The Reader This Book Is Written For

This book is for the reader who is already beyond the introductory question of whether AI matters.

It is for the executive who must decide what to fund and what to challenge.
It is for the sponsor who must justify investment with more than optimism.

It is for the project or program leader who must structure delivery under uncertainty.
It is for the product owner who must balance usefulness, control, and adoption.
It is for the architect or platform leader who must connect capability to operational reality.
It is for governance, risk, procurement, legal, compliance, and audit stakeholders who must help the organization move responsibly rather than simply say yes or no from the sidelines.
It is for leaders who understand that AI is not just a technical shift, but an enterprise management problem.

Most of all, it is for the organization trying to move from scattered AI activity toward disciplined AI outcomes.

Why This Gap Matters Now

The need for this kind of playbook is becoming more urgent, not less.

AI capabilities are improving rapidly. vendors are embedding them into enterprise platforms at increasing speed. Internal pressure to "do something with AI" is intensifying. expectations are rising faster than management maturity. In that environment, organizations face a real danger: they may accelerate adoption before they have developed the discipline to govern delivery properly.

That is how waste grows.
That is how risk becomes normalized.
That is how trust is weakened.
That is how pilots multiply without scaling well.
And that is how promising AI strategies become fragmented, expensive, and hard to defend.

The right answer is not retreat.

It is better management.

That is the central purpose of this book.

From Gap to Discipline

If Chapter 1 established that traditional project management alone is not enough for AI, this chapter explains why many readers still feel under-equipped even after engaging with the broader AI book market.

The problem is not simply lack of information. It is lack of practical integration.

Organizations need a discipline that brings together governance, delivery, experimentation, business case logic, trust, control, measurement, and scale. They need a framework that can live in the real enterprise, not only in the strategy deck, innovation lab, or technical white paper. They need a way to manage AI projects as serious investments with real operating consequences.

That is what the rest of this book is designed to provide.

The chapters that follow move from principle to practice. They will show how to identify suitable AI opportunities, assess readiness, define value, structure governance, plan delivery, manage cost, engage stakeholders, measure outcomes, and scale with control. They will treat AI not as magic, not as menace, and not as a vague future force, but as a capability class that can be managed well when the enterprise brings the right discipline to the work.

That is the shift this book asks the reader to make.

Not from caution to enthusiasm.
Not from old technology to new technology.
But from fragmented AI effort to governed AI execution.

That is the gap.

And that is the work ahead.

Chapter 3

What the Enterprise AI Project Playbook Actually Means

By now, two important ideas have been established.

First, AI initiatives cannot be managed well through traditional project management alone. The nature of AI work introduces uncertainty, data dependence, experimentation, variable performance, and trust-sensitive deployment in ways that standard delivery methods do not fully address.

Second, many existing AI books still leave enterprise readers with a practical gap. They may explain AI well, inspire action, or frame the strategic opportunity, but they often do not provide a sufficiently grounded playbook for governing, delivering, and scaling AI projects under real business constraints.

That brings us to a necessary question:

What does an enterprise AI project playbook actually have to do?

The word playbook can sound simple. It can sound like a checklist, a method, a sequence of steps, or a collection of templates. Those things matter, and this book will provide practical structure. But in an enterprise context, a playbook must mean more than a binder of good intentions or a set of generic project artifacts.

For AI projects, a playbook is the discipline that connects ambition to execution. It is the operating logic that helps leaders decide which AI opportunities deserve investment, which risks must be controlled, which evidence must be produced, which roles must be accountable, and which results must be measured before scale is justified.

In this book, The Enterprise AI Project Playbook has a demanding meaning.

It does not mean a rigid formula.
It does not mean perfect execution.
It does not mean zero risk.
It does not mean the organization moves slowly.
It does not mean innovation is constrained into irrelevance.
And it does not mean every AI initiative succeeds.

It means the organization manages AI projects with enough discipline that the work is tied to real business value, governed in proportion to its risk, delivered with operational realism, measured against meaningful outcomes, and scaled only when evidence justifies confidence.

That is the standard.

This chapter defines that standard more fully.

The Playbook Begins with the Right Problem, Not the Right Technology

One of the fastest ways to mismanage AI is to begin with the technology and search afterward for a business reason to justify it.

This happens often. A new model gains attention. A vendor promotes a feature. A board asks what the organization is doing with generative AI. Leaders feel pressure to respond. A small internal group begins brainstorming possibilities. Quickly, a set of ideas emerges: copilots, summarization, search, recommendation engines, automation assistants, predictive models, synthetic content generation, decision support tools, and more.

None of this is inherently wrong. But when the initiative begins with capability fascination rather than problem clarity, the project is placed at risk before it truly starts.

The Enterprise AI Project Playbook begins somewhere else.

It begins with a problem, a constraint, an inefficiency, a decision bottleneck, a service gap, a quality issue, a cost driver, a workflow burden, or a missed opportunity that matters enough to warrant intervention. It begins by asking what exactly needs to improve, for whom, under what conditions, and with what evidence of benefit. It asks whether AI is the right answer, not merely an available one.

That distinction is foundational.

AI can make weak problem framing more dangerous, not less. A vague problem paired with powerful technology often creates attractive motion without meaningful progress. The outputs may look sophisticated. The language may sound innovative. But the initiative may still lack a clear reason to exist.

The playbook therefore requires business clarity before technical enthusiasm is allowed to dominate. The question is not, Where can we put AI? The question is, What enterprise problem are we solving, and why is AI an appropriate and defensible way to solve it?

Until that is clear, the initiative is not yet ready.

The Playbook Treats Use Cases as Investment Decisions

Not every plausible AI use case deserves to move forward.

That truth may sound obvious, yet many organizations behave as though the mere identification of an AI opportunity is enough to justify momentum. It is not. A long list of promising ideas is not a pipeline of viable investments. It is only a starting pool.

The playbook requires choice.

That choice must be disciplined. It must consider expected value, implementation feasibility, data readiness, operational impact, control burden, adoption risk, reputational sensitivity, policy implications, and measurable return. It must distinguish between what is technically possible and what is enterprise-ready. It must recognize that some use cases should be piloted narrowly, some redesigned, some sequenced later, and some declined entirely.

This is where many AI efforts begin to diverge.

Poorly managed organizations treat use cases as opportunity theater. They collect them, present them, celebrate them, and sometimes fund them without sufficient scrutiny. Well-managed organizations treat use cases as investment propositions. They evaluate them with seriousness. They ask what conditions must be true before they are worth pursuing. They consider not only the upside of success, but the burden of governing, sustaining, and defending the capability once it exists.

That is what an enterprise playbook requires.

It is not anti-innovation. It is anti-naivety.

The Playbook Forces Data Realism Early

If a business case is built on weak data assumptions, the project is already compromised.

This is one of the most important distinctions between AI initiative quality and AI initiative theater. In poorly governed efforts, data problems are often acknowledged in general terms but deferred in practice. Teams assume the data will be cleaned up later, made available, connected during implementation, or good enough for a pilot. Sometimes that optimism survives long enough to fund the initiative. It rarely survives contact with operational reality.

The playbook does not romanticize data.

It asks early whether the relevant data exists, whether it is accessible, whether it is current enough, consistent enough, governed enough, and representative enough to support the intended outcome. It asks who owns it, who can authorize its use, what exceptions exist, what quality issues are known, what labels or historical signals are missing, and what dependencies on upstream systems may undermine the initiative later.

This matters because AI projects are often not defeated by model limitations first. They are defeated by the condition of the surrounding information environment.

The playbook does not wait until build is underway to discover that foundational data is fragmented, ambiguous, stale, contradictory, politically sensitive, or simply unusable at the level the use case requires. It confronts those realities early enough to change scope, sequence, cost assumptions, timelines, or even the go-no-go decision itself.

This is not pessimism. It is maturity.

The Playbook Builds Learning into the Delivery Model

Organizations often say they want innovation, but what they really want is certainty disguised as innovation.

They want AI to behave like a conventional software feature: scoped cleanly, planned confidently, built predictably, tested crisply, and delivered with little ambiguity. In practice, AI rarely offers that comfort at the beginning.

The initiative may need experimentation. It may need comparative testing. It may require threshold discovery. It may reveal that an assumed workflow needs redesign. It may show that a use case framed as automation should really be deployed as decision support. It may uncover error patterns that force reconsideration of oversight. It may produce partial value rather than full automation value.

The playbook does not hide that.

It does not pretend that genuine uncertainty has already been resolved. Nor does it let experimentation drift into loose, endless exploration with no discipline. It governs learning. It defines what is being tested, why, how results will be interpreted, who makes the decision to proceed, and what evidence is required before moving into broader commitment.

This is a critical point.

The Enterprise AI Project Playbook does not require certainty from day one. It requires uncertainty to be managed honestly, intentionally, and with control. It means the project plan reflects reality rather than wishful sequencing. It means sponsors are not misled into believing the path is more fixed than it really is. It means experiments produce decision-quality evidence, not just interesting artifacts.

A mature AI delivery model does not erase learning. It structures it.

The Playbook Defines Success in Terms That Fit AI

Many projects fail quietly because they use the wrong definition of success.

In traditional delivery, success may be measured through familiar indicators: delivered on time, delivered on budget, requirements met, defects resolved, training completed, go-live achieved. These remain important, but AI initiatives demand more.

A technically launched AI capability can still be a management failure. It may operate inconsistently. It may require more human correction than expected. It may erode trust. It may create savings in one area while creating burden in another. It may produce outputs that are plausible but not reliable enough. It may technically meet launch criteria while failing to improve the actual decision, service, or process it was intended to enhance.

The playbook does not confuse implementation completion with enterprise success.

It defines success more carefully. It asks whether the capability is producing meaningful business improvement. Whether it is usable in real operating conditions. Whether it is controlled appropriately. Whether users understand when to rely on it and when to escalate. Whether its performance is strong enough for the context in which it is deployed. Whether the economics remain credible after operational realities are included. Whether leaders would still support the initiative if all hidden overheads were made visible.

These are harder questions than, Did it launch?

That is precisely why they matter.

The Playbook Builds Governance In, Not Around

Governance is often mishandled in one of two ways.

In some organizations, governance arrives too late. The project moves forward in the language of speed and experimentation until the initiative becomes visible enough to trigger concern. Then legal, compliance, risk, audit, privacy, security, or executive stakeholders enter the conversation abruptly. Questions emerge that were never answered. Ownership is unclear. Documentation is thin. Controls are partial. Confidence drops.

In other organizations, governance is so abstract or disconnected that it becomes a brake rather than an enabler. Teams hear principles but do not know what they mean operationally. Review becomes episodic. Expectations are unclear. Approval logic feels improvised.

The playbook avoids both failures.

It does not treat governance as something wrapped around the project after technical enthusiasm has already set direction. And it does not treat governance as a vague collection of values with no operational translation. It builds governance into the delivery model from the start.

That means decision rights are clearer. Risk classification happens earlier. Review checkpoints are known. Escalation paths exist. Human oversight is intentionally designed. Documentation is proportional to the stakes. Evidence is preserved. Boundaries are defined. Control expectations are visible to delivery teams while there is still time to act on them.

Good governance does not exist to frustrate AI progress. It exists to make enterprise progress sustainable.

The playbook understands that scale depends on this.

The Playbook Treats Trust as a Design Requirement

Trust is sometimes discussed as though it were a secondary concern to be handled through training, messaging, or change management after the system is built.

That is not enough.

In AI initiatives, trust is often one of the most decisive conditions of success. If users do not trust the outputs, they will work around the system or ignore it. If managers do not trust the recommendations, they will not rely on them. If executives do not trust the controls, they will hesitate to expand the investment. If legal, compliance, audit, or external stakeholders do not trust the governance, the organization will eventually pay the price.

The playbook does not leave trust to chance.

It treats trust as something that must be designed for. That includes explainability where appropriate, transparency about boundaries, sensible escalation paths, clear human accountability, reliable performance monitoring, defensible review processes, and alignment between what the system claims to do and what it can truly do under operational conditions.

This matters because AI can generate a dangerous illusion of confidence. It can sound polished, coherent, and helpful while still being incomplete, inconsistent, or wrong in ways that matter. Trust, therefore, cannot be based on fluency alone. It must be earned through controlled usefulness and visible accountability.

The playbook understands that trust is not the public-relations layer of AI. It is one of the operating conditions under which AI can create value.

The Playbook Keeps Humans in the Management Loop, Not Just the Workflow

Human-in-the-loop is one of the most frequently invoked phrases in enterprise AI. It is also one of the most misunderstood.

Sometimes it is treated as a blanket reassurance. A system is considered acceptable simply because a human is somewhere in the process. But that alone says very little. The real questions are more demanding. Where is the human in the process? What are they expected to review? What authority do they retain? What information do they have to exercise judgment? What volume can they realistically handle? What happens when they disagree with the output? What happens when they become fatigued or over-reliant?

The playbook does not use humans as symbolic control points.

It defines human roles carefully. It distinguishes between oversight that is meaningful and oversight that is merely decorative. It recognizes that some decisions require active review, some require exception handling, some require spot-checking, and some should remain fully human-led despite AI assistance. It also recognizes that poor human oversight design can create its own risks: bottlenecks, rubber-stamping, fatigue, and false confidence.

This is where mature AI management differs from superficial assurance language. The playbook asks not merely whether a human is involved, but whether the human role is operationally credible.

The Playbook Includes Cost Realism, Not Just Innovation Ambition

Many AI initiatives are approved under a haze of innovation optimism. The potential upside is discussed energetically. The cost picture is often thinner.

That imbalance is dangerous.

The Enterprise AI Project Playbook requires cost realism from the start. Not only implementation cost, but operational cost. Not only licensing or platform fees, but monitoring, human review, retraining or tuning effort, prompt and evaluation work, governance overhead, integration support, maintenance, vendor dependence, and the hidden expense of exception handling. It asks where costs may rise with usage, where quality requires staffing, where technical complexity creates maintenance burden, and where a successful capability may still have weak economics.

This does not mean organizations should avoid AI initiatives with meaningful investment needs. It means those needs should be understood honestly.

An AI project is not governed well if it creates apparent productivity gains while quietly shifting labor, risk, or cost into places the business case did not count. It is not enterprise-ready if pilot economics are used to justify scale without re-examining what scale will truly cost. It is not investment-grade if leaders celebrate novelty before they understand the total operating model required to support it.

The playbook respects the budget not as an administrative constraint, but as part of enterprise truth.

The Playbook Plans for Operational Ownership Before Launch

One of the most common signs of immature AI management is that the initiative approaches launch before anyone can clearly answer a simple question:

Who owns this once it is live?

The answers are often partial. IT owns the platform. The business owns the outcome. Data owns the information source. Compliance owns the policy. Operations owns the workflow. A product team owns enhancements. A vendor owns part of the underlying capability. Each answer contains some truth, yet the whole remains unclear.

The playbook resolves that before deployment.

It defines who owns performance, who owns monitoring, who reviews exceptions, who can approve changes, who tracks value realization, who handles policy incidents, who manages knowledge updates, who is accountable for adoption health, and who decides when the capability should be expanded, constrained, redesigned, or withdrawn.

This is essential because AI projects do not end cleanly at go-live. They enter a different phase of responsibility. Without clear ownership, drift begins. Costs become harder to interpret. Trust signals weaken. Errors get normalized. Escalations wander. The system remains active while accountability diffuses.

The playbook does not allow that handoff ambiguity to remain unresolved. It knows that operational ownership is part of project quality, not a separate issue to solve later.

The Playbook Scales Only When Evidence Justifies It

Premature scaling is one of the costliest mistakes in AI.

The organization sees enough early promise to become eager. A pilot looks encouraging. User reaction is positive. Executive attention rises. Vendor enthusiasm adds momentum. The initiative begins to gather symbolic significance inside the organization. Suddenly the pressure shifts from learning to expansion.

This is precisely the moment discipline matters most.

The playbook does not scale because excitement is high. It scales because evidence is strong enough. It asks whether the capability has performed well across meaningful scenarios, whether control mechanisms have been tested, whether adoption is holding under real usage, whether cost behavior remains acceptable, whether operational teams can support the broader rollout, whether policy questions have been answered, and whether the system has proven itself beyond the curated conditions of early experimentation.

Scaling without that evidence can multiply weaknesses faster than it multiplies benefits.

The playbook is not anti-scale. It is pro-defensible scale.

The Playbook Makes Enterprise Discipline Visible

At this point, a pattern should be clear.

The Enterprise AI Project Playbook is not one feature of a project. It is not one checkpoint. It is not one committee approval. It is not one pilot success. It is not a vendor claim. It is not a tone of seriousness.

It is the visible presence of enterprise discipline across the life of the initiative.

It is visible in how the problem is framed.
It is visible in how use cases are chosen.
It is visible in how data readiness is confronted.
It is visible in how experimentation is governed.
It is visible in how success is defined.
It is visible in how trust is designed for.
It is visible in how cost is understood.

It is visible in how governance is embedded.
It is visible in how ownership is assigned.
It is visible in how scale is earned.

This is why the title matters.

Without a clear playbook, organizations may believe they are managing AI responsibly when they are merely moving carefully around an unclear core. The playbook gives the book a standard against which decisions can be tested. It creates a benchmark for judging whether the initiative is truly being governed, delivered, and scaled in a way that is worthy of enterprise trust and capable of producing measurable ROI.

What the Playbook Does Not Mean

It is worth stating explicitly what this playbook does not require.

It does not require that every decision be slow.
It does not require that innovation be buried in committee review.
It does not require that uncertainty be eliminated before work begins.
It does not require that every pilot be over-engineered.
It does not require that only low-risk, low-value use cases be attempted.
And it does not require that organizations wait for perfect maturity before taking action.

The Enterprise AI Project Playbook is not perfectionism.

It is proportionate seriousness.

It means the level of discipline matches the level of consequence. It means the organization knows the difference between testing an internal drafting aid and deploying a high-impact decision support capability. It means controls are calibrated to stakes. It means speed is used intelligently rather than recklessly. It means learning happens, but not without boundaries. It means ambition exists, but not without accountability.

In other words, the playbook is not an argument against movement. It is an argument against unmanaged movement.

The Definition This Book Will Use Going Forward

For the remainder of this book, we will use a practical definition:

The Enterprise AI Project Playbook is the disciplined management framework for selecting, governing, delivering, measuring, and scaling AI projects so they solve real business problems, operate within clear risk boundaries, produce decision-quality evidence, earn user and stakeholder trust, and create measurable ROI over time.

That definition will guide the chapters ahead.

It will shape how we think about use case selection.
It will shape how we think about readiness.
It will shape how we think about governance.
It will shape how we think about funding and ROI.
It will shape how we think about stakeholder alignment.
It will shape how we think about deployment, adoption, and scale.

Without that standard, AI project management becomes vague very quickly. With it, leaders gain a more practical way to judge what should move forward, what should be reworked, what needs stronger controls, and what is not yet ready.

The Work Ahead

The rest of this book is an attempt to make that definition usable.

Not inspirational only.

Not theoretical only.

Usable.

Because enterprises do not need another reminder that AI is important. They already know that. What they need is a way to move from pressure to discipline, from scattered experimentation to managed execution, and from possibility to provable results.

That is what The Enterprise AI Project Playbook is meant to provide.

It is the difference between launching something impressive and building something sustainable.

It is the difference between AI activity and AI accountability.

It is the difference between temporary momentum and enterprise value.

And once that standard is clear, the next question becomes unavoidable:

How should an organization decide which AI opportunities are actually worth pursuing in the first place? That is where we go next.

Part 2 – Choosing the Right AI Projects

Chapter 4

Selecting AI Use Cases Worth Doing

This chapter provides a disciplined framework for choosing the right AI opportunities. Its purpose is to help leaders avoid low-value experimentation and focus investment on use cases with a credible path to enterprise value. That means looking beyond novelty and technical promise alone. A worthwhile AI use case must show business value, feasible delivery conditions, sufficient data readiness, manageable operational complexity, acceptable risk, reasonable process maturity, and a change burden the organization can actually absorb.

Not Every AI Use Case Deserves to Be Pursued

One of the most expensive mistakes organizations make in AI is not technical failure. It is poor selection.

Teams often begin with enthusiasm, vendor demos, executive curiosity, or a broad belief that AI should be applied somewhere. The result is a growing list of possible use cases, proof-of-concept ideas, and pilot candidates. On the surface, this can look like progress. It signals momentum. It creates the appearance of innovation. But without disciplined selection, it quickly becomes costly noise.

Some AI opportunities are too vague to operationalize. Some depend on weak or inaccessible data. Some create value in theory but do not survive the realities of trust, governance, integration, or change adoption. Some can be piloted successfully but cannot be supported economically at scale. Others appear strategic but are attached to immature processes that are not stable enough to benefit from AI in the first place.

This is why choosing the right AI projects is not a lightweight front-end exercise. It is one of the most important management decisions in the entire lifecycle.

A good selection process does more than identify appealing ideas. It filters for delivery-worthy ideas. It asks not only whether AI might help, but whether the use case has a credible path to business value, enterprise adoption, and controlled execution.

The First Selection Error: Confusing Interest with Worth

In many organizations, AI use cases enter the pipeline for the wrong reasons. They are selected because the problem is visible, because a senior leader mentioned it, because a vendor showcased a similar example, because the task appears repetitive, or because competitors are rumored to be doing something related. None of these signals is meaningless, but none is sufficient.

The question is not whether a use case is interesting. The question is whether it is worth doing.

A use case worth doing has several characteristics at once. It addresses a real business problem. It has identifiable value. It depends on data that can realistically be accessed and prepared. It fits a process mature enough to support intervention. It operates within an acceptable risk boundary. It does not create change burden so great that adoption collapses. And it has a plausible path from experiment to enterprise delivery.

That last point matters. In Chapter 1, the distinction was conceptual: AI product discovery is not the same as enterprise AI delivery. In this chapter, that distinction becomes a selection rule. A promising hypothesis is not yet a good project. A feasible proof of concept is not yet a sound enterprise investment. A use case should be selected only when leadership can see how it could move from AI hypothesis to controlled business use.

This chapter therefore treats selection not as brainstorming, but as investment discipline.

What Makes an AI Use Case Worth Doing

A worthwhile AI use case sits at the intersection of seven conditions: **business value, technical feasibility, data readiness, operational fit, acceptable risk, process maturity, and manageable change burden.**

If one of these is materially absent, the initiative may still be interesting, but it is probably not ready for responsible investment.

Business value asks whether the use case solves a problem that matters enough to justify funding, leadership attention, and organizational effort. The value may come through cost reduction, service improvement, risk reduction, speed, consistency, quality, revenue lift, or decision support. But it must be identifiable and meaningful.

Technical feasibility asks whether current methods can plausibly deliver the needed outcome at a useful level of performance. This is not the same as asking whether a model can produce output. The real question is whether the output can perform reliably enough, in context, for the business to act on it.

Data readiness asks whether the required data exists, can be accessed lawfully, is sufficiently reliable, and can support the intended use. In many AI programs, this is the hidden gate that decides the fate of the project before the team fully realizes it.

Operational fit asks whether the use case belongs in a real workflow. If the output does not fit how people work, how decisions are made, or how systems interact, the use case will struggle even if the model is technically sound.

Acceptable risk asks whether the potential errors, biases, exposures, or compliance implications can be managed within the organization's control structure. Some use cases look attractive until their downside is examined honestly.

Process maturity asks whether the underlying business process is stable enough to benefit from AI. Automating or augmenting a broken, undefined, or inconsistently executed process rarely creates durable value.

Manageable change burden asks whether the organization can realistically absorb the changes required for adoption. If the use case demands new roles, major behavior shifts, unclear accountability, or trust the user base is not prepared to grant, the initiative may stall regardless of technical promise.

A use case worth doing is rarely perfect in all seven categories. But it should be credible in all of them.

A Practical Risk Approach for Getting Started

Organizations do not need a perfect AI risk methodology before they begin selecting use cases. But they do need more than intuition, vendor enthusiasm, or executive curiosity. The goal at this stage is not to perform a full legal, regulatory, or model-governance review for every idea. The goal is to apply enough structured discipline to separate credible opportunities from costly distractions.

The approach in this chapter is designed as a practical starting point. It is informed by several established methods. From **BXT** it borrows the idea that a use case must be viable commercially, usable in practice, and feasible technically. From a **use case prioritization matrix**, it borrows the discipline of weighing business value against complexity and risk. From **NIST AI RMF**, it borrows the principle that AI risk must be governed, mapped, measured, and managed rather than treated as an afterthought. From **pre-mortem**

simulation and **SWIFT analysis**, it borrows the discipline of challenging optimistic assumptions before commitment. From **algorithm impact assessment**, it borrows the need to examine accuracy, bias, privacy, and consequence before adoption. From the **three horizons approach**, it borrows the recognition that risks emerge across immediate, medium-term, and strategic timescales. From **red-yellow-green risk categorization**, it borrows the idea that not all AI use cases deserve the same tolerance, speed, or governance burden.

This chapter does not reproduce those methods in full. It translates their most useful front-end disciplines into a practical selection method leaders can use immediately. Its purpose is to help organizations start well.

Exhibit 4A — Risk-Adjusted AI Use Case Screening Method

Step	Core question	What to examine
1. Define the use case	What exactly are we trying to do?	Problem clarity, intended user, workflow or decision affected, expected value, consequence of error
2. Assess attractiveness	Is this worth pursuing?	Business value, strategic relevance, speed to benefit, repeatability of value
3. Assess feasibility and readiness	Can this be delivered credibly?	Data readiness, technical feasibility, process maturity, operational fit, change burden
4. Assess exposure	What could go wrong if we choose this?	Financial waste, governance and compliance exposure, operational disruption, trust damage, opportunity cost
5. Determine posture	What should we do now?	Priority Now, Advance Carefully, Defer, or Avoid

The Risk of Choosing the Wrong AI Use Case

Selecting the wrong AI use case creates more than a failed pilot. It creates wasted spend, governance strain, portfolio drag, trust erosion, and delayed value elsewhere. For that reason, AI use case selection should be treated as a risk-adjusted investment decision.

At this stage, organizations do not need an overly elaborate scoring regime. They need a disciplined method for getting started. That method should force the team to ask not only whether the use case is attractive, but whether it is worth its cost, burden, and exposure.

The wrong AI use case is not always one that fails technically. Sometimes it works technically and still becomes the wrong choice because the business value is too small, the data burden is too high, the governance burden is too heavy, the process is too immature, the support cost destroys the ROI, or the solution cannot scale under control.

The most useful front-end risk categories are these:

Financial exposure. What will it cost to prepare data, build, integrate, govern, train, monitor, tune, and support the use case? How much of that spend is at risk if the use case stalls?

Governance and compliance exposure. Does the use case touch regulated decisions, sensitive data, employee records, customer communications, approvals, or auditable workflows?

Operational exposure. What happens if the system is wrong, inconsistent, unavailable, or poorly adopted in production?

Trust and reputation exposure. Will users rely on it? Will managers defend it? Will weak early performance damage confidence in future AI efforts?

Opportunity exposure. What stronger use cases will be delayed because this one consumed budget, attention, and delivery capacity?

Exhibit 4B — Practical Risk Posture for AI Use Case Selection

Posture	Meaning	Typical profile
Priority Now	Strong candidate for early action	High value, credible feasibility, manageable exposure, sufficient control readiness
Advance Carefully	Worth pursuing with defined controls	Good value, but governance, data, or change risks need active mitigation
Defer	Promising, but not ready	Attractive idea held back by weak data, immature process, or low control readiness
Avoid	Poor current investment	Low value, high exposure, weak feasibility, or unacceptable consequence of failure

Worked Example: AI for Service Desk Ticket Triage and Resolution Recommendation

The selection method becomes easier to understand when it is applied to a realistic enterprise case.

Assume a mid-size enterprise is considering an AI use case for its IT service desk. The proposed solution would classify incoming tickets, assign likely urgency and business impact, route tickets to the correct resolver group, recommend a knowledge article or draft response for the agent, and automate a small subset of routine requests such as password resets.

This looks attractive because manual support ticket management is frequently inefficient. In this example, roughly **35 percent of tickets are misrouted**, critical tickets often sit in the same queue as low-priority tasks, and unnecessary escalations consume higher-cost staff time. The service desk also knows that delayed acknowledgment and poor triage increase the risk of SLA breaches and user dissatisfaction.

Step 1 — Define the use case clearly

The problem is not "apply AI to the service desk." The business problem must be defined more precisely.

Business problem: tickets are often misrouted, inconsistently prioritized, and handled too slowly, creating longer resolution times, higher support cost, and more escalations.

AI hypothesis: if AI can reduce misrouting, improve prioritization, and recommend the right next action or knowledge article, agents will resolve issues faster and with greater consistency.

Intended users: service desk agents, dispatchers, and support managers.

Workflow affected: ticket triage, routing, prioritization, knowledge recommendation, and early-stage resolution handling.

Consequence of error: delays, misrouting, unresolved tickets, missed incidents, SLA failures, and loss of trust in the tool.

Step 2 — Assess attractiveness

Assume the current service desk handles **10,000 tickets per month**.

Current conditions:

- **35% misrouted tickets = 3,500 tickets per month**
- average manual triage time = **5 minutes per ticket**
- average rework from misrouting = **12 additional minutes per misrouted ticket**
- about **20% of misrouted tickets** are unnecessarily escalated to higher-tier support = **700 tickets per month**

- each unnecessary escalation consumes about **20 minutes of higher-tier staff time**
- current first-contact resolution rate = **58%**
- current SLA miss rate = **14%**

For cost illustration, assume:

- Level 1 service desk labor cost = **$38/hour**
- blended rework labor cost across tiers = **$55/hour**
- Level 2 or specialist labor cost = **$80/hour**

This is enough to show why the use case attracts attention. The problem is real, visible, high-volume, and operationally meaningful.

Step 3 — Assess feasibility and readiness

This is where the use case becomes more complicated.

Historical tickets may be mislabeled, inconsistently categorized, duplicated, or missing clean resolution data. Resolver groups may have changed over time. Priority rules may not have been applied consistently. Knowledge articles may be outdated, incomplete, or poorly linked to actual ticket outcomes.

The process may also be less mature than leaders assume. If the service desk has inconsistent triage rules, weak knowledge management, unclear ownership, or frequent exceptions, the AI will inherit that disorder rather than solve it.

Operational fit is not automatic either. Agents still need to understand when to accept, question, or override the AI's recommendation. Without clear human-in-the-loop rules, the tool may create confusion rather than speed.

Step 4 — Assess exposure

Now the full risk picture emerges.

Financial exposure is broader than the model or license. It includes process review, ticket analysis, taxonomy cleanup, knowledge remediation, integration, testing, training, monitoring, tuning, and support.

Governance exposure is moderate. Tickets may contain employee data, device data, incident information, or security-related content. Access controls, retention rules, privacy expectations, and auditability matter.

Operational exposure is moderate to high. Misclassification of routine tickets is inconvenient. Misclassification of major incidents or security issues can be serious.

Trust exposure is high. If early suggestions are weak, agents may stop using the AI altogether.

Opportunity exposure is also material. A poorly selected service desk AI project can consume budget and platform attention that might have produced greater value elsewhere.

Exhibit 4C — Completed Example: Cost and Value View for AI Service Desk Triage

Cost or value element	Monthly estimate	Annual estimate
Manual triage labor: 10,000 × 5 min	$31,667	$380,000
Misrouting rework: 3,500 × 12 min	$38,500	$462,000
Unnecessary escalations: 700 × 20 min	$18,667	$224,000
Total visible annual burden today		**$1,066,000**

This does not include user frustration, business productivity loss, managerial escalation handling, or reputation cost for IT support. It is simply the visible operating burden tied to slow, manual, and error-prone handling.

Now assume the organization invests in this use case.

Illustrative first-year investment:

Investment category	Estimate
Workflow review and use case design	$40,000
Historical ticket analysis and taxonomy cleanup	$80,000
Knowledge base cleanup and refresh	$60,000
AI configuration, integration, and testing	$180,000
Security, access controls, and governance review	$35,000

Investment category	Estimate
Change management and training	$45,000
Monitoring, tuning, and support in year one	$110,000
Total first-year investment	**$550,000**

Now assume the use case is selected well and the groundwork is done properly. The organization stabilizes ticket categories, refreshes the knowledge base, verifies training data quality, and defines override rules.

Target performance:

- misrouting improves from **35% to 15%**
- triage time drops from **5 minutes to 2 minutes**
- unnecessary escalations are reduced by **30%**

Illustrative annual benefit:

Benefit source	Annual estimate
Triage effort reduced from 5 to 2 minutes	$228,000
Misrouting reduced from 35% to 15%	$264,000
Unnecessary escalations reduced by 30%	$67,000
Total direct annual savings	**$559,000**

That means the use case may roughly cover its first-year investment and become more attractive in later years when one-time cleanup and setup costs fall away.

Now consider the bad-selection version. Leadership approves the idea too early. Ticket labels are inconsistent. Categories are unstable. Knowledge articles are stale. The pilot measures technical accuracy but not live workflow outcomes.

In that weaker scenario:

- misrouting improves only from **35% to 28%**
- triage time drops only from **5 minutes to 4 minutes**
- unnecessary escalations fall by only **10%**

Illustrative annual benefit then becomes:

Benefit source	**Annual estimate**
Triage reduction of 1 minute	$76,000
Misrouting improvement of 7 percentage points	$92,000
Escalation reduction of 10%	$22,000
Total direct annual savings	**$190,000**

Against a first-year investment of **$550,000**, the use case now produces a **negative first-year return of roughly $360,000**. That still excludes the secondary damage of continued SLA misses, extra governance burden, rework around poor data, and weaker trust in future AI initiatives.

This is the management lesson. A use case can look cheap in pilot form and still become expensive in enterprise form.

Exhibit 4D — Example Risk and Cost View: AI Service Desk Triage

Dimension	**Example finding**	**Management implication**
Business value	Meaningful if routing and resolution improve	Worth examining
Data readiness	Often weaker than assumed	Verify before funding
Process maturity	Depends on stable triage rules	Fix process before scaling
Governance exposure	Moderate, especially for sensitive tickets	Define controls early
Trust exposure	High if recommendations are weak	Pilot with oversight
Cost exposure	Much broader than model cost alone	Estimate full lifecycle cost
Overall posture	Advance Carefully	Proceed only with defined controls

In most organizations, this use case should not be classified as an automatic **Priority Now**. It is more often an **Advance Carefully** case. It has real value potential, but only if the process is stable enough, the data is usable enough, the knowledge content is current enough, and the human oversight model is clear enough.

This example shows why AI use case selection must be treated as a risk-adjusted management decision. The service desk use case appears attractive because the pain is real, the waste is visible, and the potential gains are easy to imagine. But once the numbers are examined, the true gates become visible: data quality, process maturity, governance overhead, user trust, production support cost, and the difference between pilot success and enterprise viability.

From AI Hypothesis to Enterprise AI Delivery

Chapter 1 established the distinction. This chapter applies it. Use case selection should not stop at the question, "Is this a promising AI hypothesis?" It should continue to the harder question, "Does this hypothesis have a credible path to enterprise delivery?"

Exhibit 4E — From AI Hypothesis to Enterprise AI Delivery

Stage	Core question	Selection implication
AI Hypothesis	What useful outcome might AI produce?	Start with a specific problem and a specific business effect, not generic enthusiasm
Data Preparation and Readiness	Can the needed data be sourced, accessed, prepared, and governed?	Eliminate use cases with weak, inaccessible, unstable, or high-risk data foundations
Proof of Feasibility	Can the approach perform usefully enough in controlled conditions?	Do not mistake technical possibility for business viability
Initial Production Release	Can this be integrated into live workflows with accountability and controls?	Prioritize use cases that can survive operational reality, not just test environments
Controlled Scale-Up	Can this be expanded safely, economically, and consistently?	Favor use cases with repeatable value and manageable support, oversight, and cost

The importance of this exhibit is not the sequence alone. It is the discipline it imposes. It forces leaders to choose use cases that can travel across the full path, rather than stalling at the first point of technical excitement.

A Disciplined Framework for Selecting AI Use Cases

A strong selection framework asks a set of structured questions.

Is the problem important enough?

Not every inefficiency deserves AI. Does the use case address a real operational burden, service problem, risk exposure, capacity constraint, or decision bottleneck?

Is the value clear enough to measure?
What is expected to improve: speed, quality, accuracy, throughput, resolution time, conversion, cost avoidance, or risk reduction?

Is the data ready enough to support the outcome?
Does the needed data exist, can it be accessed, and is it usable and governable for the intended purpose?

Is the process mature enough for AI intervention?
A process with undefined ownership, inconsistent execution, excessive exceptions, or unstable policy rules is rarely a strong candidate.

Is the operational complexity manageable?
What integrations, workflow changes, support expectations, and exception paths will be required?

Is the risk exposure acceptable?
What happens if the system is wrong, biased, unavailable, or misunderstood?

Is the change burden realistic?
Will users trust it? Can they be trained? Does it disrupt behavior more than the value justifies?

A use case that fails these questions may still be intellectually interesting. It is simply not ready for enterprise investment.

The Best Early AI Use Cases

In most enterprises, the best early AI use cases share a recognizable pattern. They address a meaningful but bounded problem. They rely on data that already exists or can be prepared without heroic effort. They fit a reasonably mature process. They offer value that can be measured within months, not years. They keep risk within manageable limits. And they can be introduced into real workflows without overwhelming the organization.

These are not always the most glamorous use cases. They are often more operational than visionary. But they are the use cases most likely to build trust, establish credibility, and create the evidence base needed for broader adoption later.

That matters because early use case selection shapes more than project outcomes. It shapes executive confidence, user trust, funding appetite, governance maturity, and the political future of the AI program itself.

The Wrong Use Cases to Select First

Organizations should be cautious about pursuing several types of AI use cases too early.

The first are use cases with unclear business value. If the use case sounds exciting but cannot be tied to meaningful outcomes, it should not receive scarce enterprise attention.

The second are use cases with weak or inaccessible data. Teams often underestimate how much effort will be required to gather, clean, permission, and operationalize data.

The third are use cases attached to immature processes. If the business does not understand the process well enough to describe its decisions, exceptions, and outcomes, AI will expose the confusion rather than resolve it.

The fourth are high-risk use cases without corresponding control maturity. A consequential use case may eventually be viable, but if the organization lacks the oversight model, governance discipline, or operational safeguards to manage it, it should not be an early bet.

The fifth are use cases with excessive change burden relative to likely gain. When the organizational disruption is heavy and the measurable return is still uncertain, the use case should be deferred or redesigned.

This is not a call for caution for its own sake. It is a call for sequencing. Some use cases are not bad ideas. They are simply bad first bets.

A Practical Selection Filter

For executive and sponsor discussions, it is useful to apply a simple screening filter:

Should we do it? Can we do it? Can we trust it? Can we operate it? Is it worth scaling?

These five questions quickly expose weak candidates.

Should we do it? focuses on business priority and value.
Can we do it? focuses on feasibility and data readiness.
Can we trust it? focuses on risk, explainability, oversight, and user confidence.
Can we operate it? focuses on integration, workflow fit, ownership, and support.
Is it worth scaling? focuses on economics, repeatability, and enterprise relevance.

A use case that passes only the first two is still immature. A use case worth funding should have a plausible answer to all five.

What This Means for the Project Manager, Sponsor, and Enterprise

For the project manager, choosing the right AI project is not a preliminary activity that happens before project management begins. It is part of the work itself. In AI initiatives, poor project selection can create failure before the schedule is built, before the model is tested, and before the first stakeholder workshop is held. The project manager must therefore be involved early enough to help the organization determine whether the proposed AI initiative is worth doing, ready to begin, and capable of producing measurable value.

The project manager's role is to bring discipline to the point where enthusiasm often outruns evidence. They help translate an AI idea into a structured decision: What business problem are we solving? Is AI truly the right solution? Is the data usable? Is the process mature enough? Who owns the outcome? What risks must be governed? What evidence will prove that the project should continue, scale, pause, or stop?

For the sponsor, this means AI project approval cannot be based only on strategic ambition, competitive pressure, or executive interest. The sponsor must own the business outcome, not merely approve the technology effort. A sponsor who funds an AI initiative but does not own the workflow change, adoption challenge, value target, and governance expectations leaves the project exposed. AI value is realized in operations, not in the model alone.

For the enterprise, this means AI project selection must become a governed portfolio decision, not a collection of disconnected experiments. The organization needs a repeatable way to evaluate use cases by business value, data readiness, process maturity, operational complexity, risk, adoption burden, and measurable return. Without that discipline, the enterprise may fund pilots that generate activity but not value.

This is where the project manager becomes essential. The project manager does not replace the sponsor, data scientist, architect, risk officer, or business owner. Instead, the project manager connects them through a decision process that forces clarity before commitment. They make sure the organization does not confuse an impressive AI demo with a scalable business solution.

In practical terms, the project manager helps the enterprise move from asking:

"Where can we use AI?"

to asking:

"Where should we use AI, why does it matter, are we ready, and what evidence will prove it is worth scaling?"

That shift is one of the defining responsibilities of AI project management.

Red Flags

- The use case sounds impressive but has no clear value metric
- The data needed is assumed to exist, but has not been verified
- The process is inconsistent, undefined, or politically contested
- The use case depends on major user behavior change with little adoption planning
- The downside of error is high, but control design is vague
- The use case looks easy in demo form but requires complex integration in reality
- The expected benefit is small relative to delivery and support burden
- The use case can produce a proof of concept, but there is no credible path to production
- The pilot economics look attractive only because governance, support, and rework costs were excluded
- The use case is consuming attention that a stronger candidate should receive instead

Checklist Callout — Before You Approve an AI Use Case

Confirm that the proposed use case:

- addresses a real and important business problem
- has clearly described value and success measures
- depends on data that is known, accessible, and usable
- fits a process mature enough for intervention
- has manageable delivery complexity
- falls within acceptable risk tolerance
- has a realistic adoption path
- includes a clear human-oversight model where needed

- has a plausible route from hypothesis to enterprise delivery
- is worth funding relative to competing opportunities
- includes an honest view of full lifecycle cost, not just pilot cost

Key Takeaway

The right AI use cases are not merely those that can be imagined, demonstrated, or piloted. They are the ones that can move credibly from AI hypothesis to enterprise delivery, with real value, real readiness, and real control.

The discipline of selecting the right AI use cases leads naturally to the next question: once a use case looks promising, how should the organization judge whether it is ready to advance? The next chapter turns from selection to evaluation, examining how to assess readiness, evidence, and decision quality before committing to delivery.

Chapter 5 — Building the AI Business Case

By the time an AI idea reaches the funding table, enthusiasm is no longer enough.

The organization does not need another presentation about what AI could do. It needs a disciplined argument for why this initiative should be funded now, why this use case matters more than others, what it will cost, what it is expected to return, how long it will take, what could go wrong, and how leadership will know whether it is working.

That is the purpose of the AI business case.

A use case says, "This is interesting."
A business case says, "This is worth funding."

That distinction matters. Many AI initiatives stall not because the technology is weak, but because the proposal is vague. The problem is described in broad terms. The benefits are framed as aspiration. The costs are incomplete. The risks are minimized. The timeline is optimistic. The success measures are fuzzy. The result is not investment discipline. It is innovation theater.

A strong AI business case does the opposite. It converts curiosity into accountability. It defines the problem in operational and financial terms. It establishes a baseline. It sets measurable target outcomes. It quantifies costs and expected benefits. It states assumptions openly. It identifies dependencies and risks. It gives decision-makers enough clarity to approve, defer, reshape, or reject the investment with confidence.

This is where AI shifts from novelty to management.

Current Signal — Why the Business Case Matters More Than Ever

The urgency is real. AI use is now widespread, but financial impact at enterprise scale is still uneven. McKinsey's 2025 global survey found that 88 percent of respondents reported regular AI use in at least one business function, yet only about one-third said their organizations had begun scaling AI programs, and only 39 percent reported EBIT impact at the enterprise level. BCG reported that only about 5 percent of companies are generating value from AI at scale, while nearly 60 percent report little or no impact. IBM similarly noted that only around 25 percent of AI initiatives deliver expected ROI and just 16 percent have scaled enterprise-wide.

The lesson is clear: AI adoption is not the same as AI value. Organizations do not close that gap with excitement. They close it with disciplined selection, measurable outcomes, workflow redesign, leadership ownership, governance, and proof. McKinsey identifies workflow redesign, senior leadership commitment, human validation, and KPI tracking as factors strongly associated with meaningful value realization.

Data readiness is a major reason the gap persists. IBM defines AI-ready data as data that is high-quality, accessible, and trusted, and reports that only 29 percent of technology leaders strongly agree their enterprise data meets the quality, accessibility, and security standards needed to scale generative AI efficiently. At the same time, NIST's AI Risk Management Framework emphasizes that trustworthy AI requires governance, measurement, and risk management, while OECD guidance stresses robust governance, internal capability, and workforce upskilling as central to responsible adoption.

That is why the business case is not a finance formality. It is the control point between experimentation and accountable investment.

The Business Case Has One Job

The business case has one job: to prove that the proposed AI initiative is a credible, governed, economically sensible response to a real business problem.

Not every strong use case becomes a strong business case.

A use case may be interesting but still fail because:

- the baseline is unknown
- the data is not ready
- the process is unstable
- the owners are unclear
- the benefits are soft and unmeasured
- the implementation cost is understated
- the governance burden is ignored
- the timeline is unrealistic

A sound business case filters out weak proposals before they consume money, leadership attention, and organizational trust.

Start with the Problem, Not the Technology

The first mistake in AI business cases is beginning with the tool.

"We want an AI agent."
"We want a copilot."
"We want an intelligent assistant."

None of those are business cases.

The starting point is a business problem stated in operational terms. What is broken, slow, costly, inconsistent, risky, or manual today? What consequence does that create? What objective does the organization care about enough to fund?

Strong problem statements sound like this:

- Ticket routing errors are causing rework, delays, and SLA breaches.
- Claims intake requires too much manual review, slowing cycle time and frustrating customers.
- Knowledge retrieval is fragmented, leading to repeated work and inconsistent answers.
- Manual document classification is consuming skilled labor that should be focused on higher-value exceptions.

Weak problem statements sound like this:

- We want to modernize with AI.
- We want to explore AI opportunities.
- We want to become more innovative.
- We want a proof of concept for agents.

Leadership does not fund adjectives. Leadership funds outcomes.

Define the Baseline Before You Promise Improvement

An AI business case without a baseline is just optimism.

Before benefits are projected, the organization needs to know the current state. This means measuring today's process with enough precision to compare "before" and "after."

Microsoft's guidance on AI value measurement makes the point directly: without a measurement framework, organizations cannot prove value or optimize it.

Baseline measures usually include some combination of:

- volume per month or year
- average handling time
- error rate or rework rate
- escalation rate
- SLA breach rate
- cycle time
- customer satisfaction
- employee effort
- cost per transaction
- revenue leakage or missed opportunity
- control failures or compliance exceptions

This is the chapter where discipline begins. If the current state is unknown, the initiative is not yet ready for funding approval. The first ask may need to be a short diagnostic, not a full implementation.

Define the Target Outcome in Business Terms

The target outcome should describe what success looks like in measurable language.

Not: "Improve efficiency."
But: "Reduce average triage time from 11 minutes to 3 minutes."

Not: "Enhance customer experience."
But: "Reduce first-response time by 40 percent and raise satisfaction scores from 3.8 to 4.3."

Not: "Support staff productivity."
But: "Save 1.5 minutes per case across 240,000 annual tickets."

The strongest targets are:

- specific
- measurable
- time-bound
- owned
- tied to strategic priorities

A useful discipline is to force every proposed benefit into one of four categories:

1. **Cost reduction**
   Fewer labor hours, fewer errors, lower rework, reduced contractor spend, lower support burden.
2. **Revenue gain**
   Faster sales cycles, higher conversion, improved cross-sell, better retention, more capacity to serve.
3. **Risk reduction**
   Fewer compliance failures, fewer privacy incidents, fewer control breaches, fewer costly escalations.
4. **Capacity release**
   Staff time freed for higher-value work, allowing growth or service improvement without proportional headcount growth.

Capacity release is often real, but it should not automatically be counted as cash savings unless the organization has a credible plan to redeploy, avoid hiring, or reduce external spend.

Build the Full Cost Picture

Another common failure is partial costing.

AI business cases often include software cost and maybe implementation effort, but omit the rest of the cost stack. That creates a misleading ROI and damages trust later.

A credible cost model includes the full cost of ownership:

- software licenses or platform fees
- implementation and integration

- data preparation and cleanup
- security, privacy, and legal review
- model testing and validation
- workflow redesign
- change management and training
- support and monitoring
- ongoing tuning and maintenance
- vendor management
- governance overhead
- additional infrastructure or consumption charges
- contingency for rework

IBM notes that many organizations struggle to realize ROI because investments have outpaced ROI maturity, and that deeper integration into core workflows matters more than isolated experimentation.

The real lesson is practical: the business case should not fund a shiny pilot and quietly leave the operating model unfunded.

Quantify Benefits Conservatively

Benefit estimates should be credible enough to survive challenge from finance, operations, audit, and skeptical executives.

That means three rules.

First, use internal baseline numbers wherever possible.
Do not anchor your business case on industry hype or vendor marketing.

Second, separate gross benefit from realized benefit.
If the math shows a theoretical annual savings of $1 million, but adoption, policy limits, ramp time, and exception handling mean only 60 percent will be realized in year one, then the year-one benefit is not $1 million.

Third, apply confidence discipline.

High-confidence benefits can be counted more directly. Low-confidence benefits should be discounted, staged, or labeled as upside rather than committed return.

A practical structure is:

- high-confidence benefit
- medium-confidence benefit
- strategic upside not included in committed ROI

This is how serious business cases stay credible.

State Assumptions Explicitly

A business case is only as strong as its assumptions.

Hidden assumptions are where bad approvals are born.

State them openly:

- adoption rate expected by quarter
- degree of process standardization required
- availability of clean data
- model accuracy threshold needed for deployment
- human review rates
- integration dependencies
- staffing assumptions
- policy constraints
- vendor timeline assumptions
- expected exception volume

Assumptions do not weaken the business case. They strengthen it by making the logic testable.

Address Risks Before Approval, Not After Failure

Strong AI business cases do not treat risk as a footnote.

They address risk in the same document that asks for funding.

The minimum risk treatment should cover:

- data quality risk
- privacy and security risk
- model accuracy risk
- bias or fairness concerns where relevant
- workflow failure risk
- integration risk
- change adoption risk
- vendor lock-in risk
- legal or regulatory risk
- reputational risk
- unclear ownership risk

NIST's AI RMF frames trustworthy AI as something operationalized through governance, mapping, measurement, and management, not left to hope.

A mature business case does not claim the initiative is low risk simply because the use case sounds harmless. It shows how risk will be controlled.

Phase the Investment

Not every business case should ask for full funding on day one.

In many cases, the smarter move is phased approval:

- phase 1: diagnostic and baseline validation
- phase 2: pilot or limited deployment

- phase 3: controlled rollout
- phase 4: scale based on measured results

This protects the organization from overcommitting before the basics are proven. It also improves executive confidence because funding is tied to evidence, not promises.

The best phased business cases specify:

- what each phase will cost
- what evidence each phase must produce
- what decision gate follows each phase
- what would cause continuation, redesign, or stop

That is not hesitation. That is disciplined investment.

Define Success Measures Before Funding

Success measures should be written before funding approval, not invented after launch.

At minimum, every AI business case should define:

- operational KPIs
- financial KPIs
- adoption KPIs
- risk and control KPIs
- measurement frequency
- benefit owner
- reporting owner
- review cadence

This is essential because AI can appear successful at the activity level while failing at the business level. Usage is not value. Model quality is not ROI. A pilot demo is not a control environment.

Speak Executive Language

A good business case is not written for AI enthusiasts. It is written for decision-makers.

That means the language should be clear, economical, and business-led:

- what problem is being solved
- why it matters now
- what it will cost
- what it is expected to deliver
- what assumptions it depends on
- what risks it introduces
- how success will be measured
- who is accountable

Do not make the sponsor decode technical excitement into business sense. Do that work before the proposal goes forward.

Exhibit 5A — AI Business Case Structure

A strong AI business case should contain the following sections:

1. Problem statement
What business problem exists today, and what is its operational or financial consequence?

2. Strategic alignment
Which enterprise objective, service priority, cost agenda, growth goal, or risk objective does this support?

3. Current baseline
What are the current volumes, cycle times, error rates, service levels, cost levels, or missed opportunities?

4. Proposed AI intervention
What exactly will the AI system do, and what will remain under human control?

5. Data and process readiness
Is the process stable enough? Is the data accessible, usable, and governed?

6. Cost estimate
What is the expected year-one cost and ongoing run cost?

7. Benefit estimate
What financial and operational benefits are expected, and at what confidence level?

8. Risks and controls
What could fail, and what controls will be put in place?

9. Timeline and phases
What will happen when, and what are the decision gates?

10. Success measures and ownership
How will value be measured, and who owns realization?

Exhibit 5B — Simple Benefit Formulas for AI Business Cases

Labor savings
Annual transaction volume × minutes saved per transaction ÷ 60 × loaded hourly cost × realization rate

Avoided rework
Annual errors avoided × average remediation cost × realization rate

Capacity release
Hours freed × portion actually redeployed to higher-value work

Revenue improvement
Baseline conversion or throughput × uplift × average value per unit × margin realization rate

Risk reduction
Baseline incident volume × expected reduction × average loss avoided × confidence factor

These formulas are not sophisticated finance models. They are management tools. Their purpose is to make the case visible, testable, and challengeable.

Exhibit 5C — Completed Example: AI-Assisted Ticket Triage and Routing

Consider an enterprise support organization handling **240,000 tickets per year**. Today, tickets are triaged manually. Roughly **35 percent** are misrouted, creating rework, delays, escalations, and avoidable SLA breaches. On average, each misrouted ticket consumes about **12 minutes** of avoidable rework. The organization estimates a loaded labor cost of **$41 per hour** for support operations. It also handles approximately **12,000 high-priority tickets per year**, with a current breach rate of **14 percent** for those tickets.

The proposed solution is an AI-assisted triage capability that classifies incoming tickets, recommends urgency and impact, routes them to the correct resolver group, and generates a short summary for the receiving analyst. Human override remains available during pilot and controlled production.

The target state is intentionally moderate rather than heroic. The organization expects to reduce the misroute rate from **35 percent to 20 percent**, save **1.2 minutes per ticket** through cleaner triage and summarization, and reduce the SLA breach rate on high-priority tickets from **14 percent to 9 percent**.

The year-one investment is estimated as follows:

- software and platform cost: **$135,000**
- implementation and integration: **$220,000**
- training and change management: **$45,000**
- security, testing, and contingency: **$60,000**

This produces a **total year-one cost of $460,000**.
Ongoing annual run cost is estimated at **$190,000**.

The benefit calculation is straightforward.

First, reducing the misroute rate by **15 percentage points** avoids **36,000 misroutes per year**. At **12 minutes** of rework each and **$41 per hour**, that produces an annual savings of **$295,200**.

Second, saving **1.2 minutes per ticket** across **240,000 tickets** produces an additional **$196,800** in annual labor savings.

Third, reducing the breach rate on **12,000 high-priority tickets** from **14 percent to 9 percent** avoids **600 breaches per year**. At an estimated **$140 per avoided breach** in operational and escalation impact, this creates **$84,000** in annual benefit.

That yields a **steady-state annual quantified benefit of $576,000**.

The organization assumes that year one will realize only **70 percent** of steady-state benefit because of ramp-up, adoption, and tuning. Years two and three are projected at **95 percent** of steady state.

That produces the following three-year picture:

- **Year 1 benefit:** $403,200
- **Year 2 benefit:** $547,200
- **Year 3 benefit:** $547,200

Total 3-year benefit: $1,497,600

Against that, the cost profile is:

- **Year 1 cost:** $460,000
- **Year 2 cost:** $190,000
- **Year 3 cost:** $190,000

Total 3-year cost: $840,000

The resulting **net 3-year benefit is $657,600**, producing a simple **3-year ROI of 78 percent**, with estimated payback between **month 18 and month 20**.

Exhibit 5D — Completed Business Case Snapshot

Field	Completed Example
Initiative	AI-Assisted Ticket Triage and Routing
Sponsor	VP, Enterprise Support Services
Business owner	Director, Service Operations
Investment ask	$420,000 year one
Why now	Current support model is absorbing avoidable rework, delaying urgent tickets, and contributing to rising operating cost and SLA pressure.
Expected outcomes	• Reduce ticket misrouting from approximately **35% to 15–18%** within the first year. • Reduce average agent handling time for triage-related work by **20–25%**. • Reduce SLA breaches related to routing delays by **25–30%**. • Improve urgent incident identification so that **90%+ of high-priority tickets are correctly classified during intake or first review**. • Reduce manual reassignment and rework by approximately **8,000–10,000 tickets annually**.
Financial case	• Year-one cost: **$420,000** • Ongoing annual cost: **$180,000** • Estimated year-one benefit: **$476,960** • Steady-state annual benefit: **$681,920** • 3-year ROI: **136 percent** • Payback: approximately **11 months**

Benefit ramp assumption	Year-one benefit is estimated at **$476,960**, or roughly **70 percent of steady-state annual benefit**, because the project requires time for design, pilot, training, adoption, governance approval, and operational stabilization. Full steady-state benefit of **$681,920 annually** is expected after the solution is adopted and operating consistently across the support environment. This value ramp supports the estimated **11-month payback** and helps make the ROI case more credible than assuming full benefit immediately after launch.
Go/no-go conditions	• Baseline validated • Ticket taxonomy cleaned • Pilot accuracy meets threshold • Logging and human override controls approved • Operations leader accepts benefit tracking ownership

Checklist Callout — Before You Approve the AI Business Case

Approve only when the proposal can answer all of the following:

- What exact business problem is being solved?
- What is the current baseline?
- What target outcome is expected, by when?
- What will the AI system do, and what remains under human control?
- Is the process stable and the data ready enough?
- What is the full year-one and run-cost estimate?
- Which benefits are hard-dollar, soft-dollar, capacity, or risk-related?
- Which assumptions matter most?
- What could cause the case to fail?
- What controls will reduce those risks?
- What phase gates and stop conditions exist?
- Who owns realization of value after deployment?

If these questions cannot be answered clearly, the case is not ready.

Key Takeaway

AI does not become fundable because it is impressive. It becomes fundable when the organization can show, in plain business terms, that a specific use case addresses a real problem, with credible economics, visible assumptions, controlled risk, and measurable outcomes.

That is the standard.

Anything less is not a business case. It is a pitch.

References

McKinsey & Company. *The State of AI: Global Survey 2025*. McKinsey & Company, 2025.

Boston Consulting Group. *Are You Generating Value from AI? The Widening Gap*. Boston Consulting Group, 2025.

Boston Consulting Group. *The Widening AI Value Gap*. Boston Consulting Group, 2025.

IBM Institute for Business Value. *IBM Study: CEOs Double Down on AI While Navigating Enterprise Hurdles*. IBM, 2025.

IBM. *What Is AI-Ready Data?* IBM Think.

National Institute of Standards and Technology. *Artificial Intelligence Risk Management Framework (AI RMF 1.0)*. NIST, 2023.

Organisation for Economic Co-operation and Development. *OECD AI Principles*. OECD, adopted 2019 and updated 2024.

Chapter 6

Data Readiness, Process Readiness, and the Preconditions for AI Success

Most AI projects do not fail in the pilot.

They fail later.

They fail when a promising proof of concept is placed inside a real workflow. They fail when the data is incomplete, stale, inconsistent, inaccessible, or semantically ambiguous. They fail when the process itself is unstable. They fail when exception handling is unclear, policies contradict one another, ownership is murky, and nobody has defined where humans remain in control.

That is why so much information on AI data readiness, though useful, is still incomplete.

Most of it gets the first half right. It says that data quality matters, that governance matters, that readiness should be tied to use cases, and that AI cannot scale on weak foundations. All of that is true. But much of it still treats data readiness as if it were mainly a data problem.

It is not.

It is an operating-model problem.

A strong Chapter 6 has to make that clear. AI does not enter a spreadsheet. It enters a living process. It enters decisions, approvals, service flows, knowledge work, customer interactions, and operational risk. That means the preconditions for success are broader than most data-readiness articles suggest.

Two preconditions matter at the same time: data readiness and process readiness.

Data readiness asks whether the system has the right information in the right condition.

Process readiness asks whether the workflow, controls, ownership model, and human decision boundaries are mature enough for AI to be inserted without creating confusion at scale.

Both are required.

Why This Matters More Now

AI is still evolving quickly. Models change. Retrieval patterns evolve. Vendor architectures mature. Costs shift. New attack paths appear. What looked advanced one year ago can become normal the next. That is precisely why leaders should not confuse changing tools with changing fundamentals.

The tools are evolving. The control principles are not.

Organizations still need authoritative data, clear ownership, controlled access, explainable outputs, observable pipelines, defensible decisions, and well-defined human accountability. As AI capabilities expand, these requirements become more important, not less.

In other words, the faster AI evolves, the more dangerous it becomes to treat readiness as a one-time technical setup.

What Most AI Data-Readiness Guidance Gets Right

Most guidance gets several important things right.

First, it correctly says that readiness is use-case-specific. Data that is acceptable for dashboards may be inadequate for forecasting, approval automation, or enterprise copilots.

Second, it correctly says that readiness is broader than data quality. Clean data alone is not enough. Meaning, context, lineage, governance, and accessibility matter just as much.

Third, it correctly says that readiness is continuous. AI systems absorb change immediately. Source systems evolve. Policies shift. Customer behavior changes. Documents age. If the organization cannot detect and respond to those changes, yesterday's "ready" environment becomes tomorrow's failure mode.

Those are important truths. But they are only the foundation.

What Most AI Data-Readiness Guidance Leaves Out

The first omission is process readiness.

Data readiness matters, but AI often fails because the workflow around the model is unstable. The exceptions are unclear. The approval logic is inconsistent. Different teams follow different rules. Nobody has defined what the AI is allowed to decide, recommend, or trigger on its own. Humans are nominally "in the loop," but nobody has specified when, why, or with what authority they intervene.

A system placed inside that kind of environment does not create order. It scales confusion.

The second omission is production-grade RAG.

RAG is often presented as an easier entry point for enterprise AI, and in many cases that is true. It can reduce the need for immediate custom training. It can surface value earlier. It can ground answers in enterprise sources. It can improve transparency because answers can be tied back to documents or records. For that reason, it is highly attractive for enterprise copilots, knowledge assistants, policy Q&A, internal search, and document-grounded support workflows.

But RAG is not a shortcut around governance.

RAG introduces its own pipeline: ingestion, filtering, parsing, chunking, embeddings, indexing, retrieval logic, permissions, freshness management, and ongoing evaluation. That means a weakly governed RAG system can fail in more places than a simple model-only interaction. It can retrieve the wrong source, the wrong version, the wrong chunk, the wrong permission scope, or the wrong answer with a convincing citation trail that gives false confidence.

The third omission is security and integrity risk in retrieval systems.

Many discussions of RAG emphasize convenience and relevance but say far less about poisoning, manipulation, or retrieval-layer attacks. Yet once an organization treats a knowledge layer as the basis for answers, that layer becomes part of the attack surface. A poisoned source, malicious instruction embedded in content, or compromised vector store can corrupt outputs while still appearing grounded.

The fourth omission is groundedness and citations as controls.

Too much public guidance treats citations as a user-interface feature. In production settings, they are a control. A grounded answer that points to current, authoritative source material is easier to verify, challenge, audit, and trust. An answer without that chain is much harder to defend, especially in regulated or operational settings.

The fifth omission is permission-aware retrieval and metadata discipline.

Many organizations focus on whether RAG can retrieve useful content. Fewer ask whether it can retrieve only the content that the user, team, or workflow is allowed to access. Fewer still define the metadata needed to filter by policy domain, geography, business unit, approval state, effective date, or document status. Without that discipline, knowledge systems become indiscriminate search layers wrapped in polished language.

That is not enterprise readiness.

Data Readiness Is Contextual, Not Generic

The phrase "AI-ready data" is often used as if it describes a universal state.

It does not.

Data is ready only in relation to a use case, a decision scope, a workflow, and a risk tolerance. A dataset that is sufficient for trend reporting may be unusable for real-time routing. A large document library may look impressive, but if it contains conflicting policy versions, unclear ownership, weak access control, and no freshness discipline, it is not ready for a knowledge assistant that employees will trust.

This is why leaders should stop asking, "Are we AI-ready?" and start asking better questions.

Ready for what use case?
Ready for what level of autonomy?
Ready for what consequence of failure?
Ready for what class of decision?
Ready under what operating conditions?

Those questions force the organization to move from abstraction to reality.

Exhibit 6A — The Two Preconditions for AI Success

Data readiness means the source is authoritative, the data is accessible, the meaning is consistent, the information is current enough, the lineage is visible, the usage is governed, and the environment is continuously monitored.

Process readiness means the workflow is stable enough, decision rights are defined, exception paths are known, human intervention points are explicit, escalation rules exist, policy conflicts are resolved, and value and risk owners are named.

If either side is weak, the system may still demo well and still fail in production.

Process Readiness Is the Missing Half

This is where Chapter 6 should be stronger than most external material.

An AI system should not be inserted into a process that nobody fully understands. It should not be used to "standardize" a workflow that has unresolved contradictions. It should not be expected to create clean operating logic where none exists.

A process is not ready for AI when the exception rate is high and undocumented, approvals differ by team or manager, policy language conflicts across sources, the workflow changes too often to stabilize, there is no clear fallback path, or nobody owns the business decision if the model is wrong.

In those conditions, even strong data will not save the use case.

This matters especially for automation-oriented AI. A knowledge assistant can often fail safely if it cites sources, signals uncertainty, and routes questions to a human. A routing, approval, or action system carries much less room for ambiguity. Its workflow boundaries must be defined before the AI arrives, not after the first incident.

What Makes Data Actually Ready

For enterprise AI, data readiness is not perfection. It is fitness for accountable use.

That means the organization can answer basic but consequential questions.

Which source is authoritative?
What does this field mean across systems?
How current is the information?
What changed upstream?
Who owns it?
Who can access it?
Can the output be traced back to source?
Can the answer be challenged and verified?

If the answer to those questions is vague, the data is not ready, even if it is plentiful.

A mature definition of readiness therefore includes source authority, semantic consistency, operational accessibility, representative coverage, traceability, stewardship, and continuous qualification over time.

That is the difference between data that exists and data that can support a real AI system.

Exhibit 6B — Seven Tests of Data Readiness

A use case should not move beyond pilot unless leadership can answer yes to most of these.

First, do we know which systems or repositories are authoritative for this use case?

Second, do key terms and fields mean the same thing across teams and systems?

Third, can the AI retrieve only what the user or process is allowed to see?

Fourth, is the information current enough for the decision being made?

Fifth, can outputs be traced back to source documents, records, or transformations?

Sixth, are the pipelines dependable enough for the workflow's tolerance for latency and failure?

Seventh, do we continuously monitor drift, content aging, source changes, and broken ingestion?

If not, the issue is not model weakness. It is environmental unreadiness.

The Role of RAG

The right way to frame RAG in this chapter is simple:

RAG is not a substitute for data readiness. It is a governed way to get earlier value from partially mature data.

That is its strength.

RAG can help organizations avoid premature custom training. It can create earlier value from existing repositories. It can improve transparency because answers can be linked to sources instead of being produced from the model alone. It can be an effective first step for policy assistants, knowledge copilots, service-support tools, legal research helpers, onboarding assistants, and other retrieval-centered use cases.

But RAG only deserves trust when the organization has solved seven things: authoritative sources, access control, ingestion discipline, chunking and parsing quality, retrieval quality, freshness management, and citation-backed monitoring.

Without those, RAG is not an enterprise knowledge layer. It is a fragile search wrapper with fluent language.

That distinction matters because many organizations are attracted to RAG precisely because it appears easier than custom model development. In one sense, it is easier. But it is easier only if the organization accepts a different burden: governance at the retrieval layer.

Why Production-Grade RAG Is Harder Than It Looks

A pilot RAG solution can appear successful very quickly. A small set of curated documents is indexed. Queries are tuned. Results look useful. Stakeholders are impressed.

That is not the same thing as production readiness.

Production-grade RAG has to solve document ingestion at scale, parsing quality for PDFs, tables, scans, and mixed formats, chunking strategy, metadata design, source filtering, duplicate and conflict management, document lifecycle control, permission enforcement, freshness and re-indexing rules, evaluation of retrieval quality, monitoring of groundedness, response behavior when retrieval is weak or conflicting, and security hardening against poisoning and prompt-injection pathways.

This is why many public treatments of RAG are too optimistic. They describe the architecture but not the operating burden.

The organization is not merely connecting documents to a model. It is building a governed information supply chain.

Before an AI System Is Trusted in Production

Before an AI system is trusted in production, leaders should ask a more practical question than whether the data is merely "available." They should ask what it will cost to get the data and workflow ready, what it will cost if they do not, and which path creates the more defensible result.

This is where data readiness stops being a technical discussion and becomes an executive risk, cost, and value decision.

Exhibit 6C — RAG Readiness Checklist

Before approving a RAG-based use case, confirm that the following are defined.

- The knowledge scope is clear: which sources are in scope, which are out of scope, and which source wins when versions conflict.

- The content controls are clear: owner for each source domain, effective date and review date, draft versus approved status, and archival and deletion rules.

- The retrieval design is clear: parsing method, chunking strategy, metadata model, index and reranking approach, citation format, and fallback behavior.

- The access controls are clear: role-aware or user-aware retrieval, handling of confidential and regulated content, and audit logging of retrieval and answer generation.

- The quality controls are clear: retrieval relevance testing, groundedness testing, citation verification, freshness monitoring, and response behavior under uncertainty.

- The security controls are clear: source allow-lists, poisoning defenses, injection-aware evaluation, and change approval for sensitive corpora.

If these are missing, the organization is not really doing enterprise RAG. It is improvising retrieval.

Exhibit 6D — The Cost of Getting Data Right vs. the Cost of Getting Data Wrong

AI data readiness is often misread as a preparatory delay or an architecture tax. In reality, it is usually a choice between paying a visible cost before launch or paying a larger, messier cost after launch.

The difference is not theoretical.

When the data is prepared properly, the organization pays upfront for source rationalization, metadata, ownership, permissions, parsing quality, retrieval quality, monitoring, and fallback design. That cost is real, but it is planned, bounded, and tied to a controlled deployment.

When the data is not prepared properly, the organization still pays. It pays in rework, escalations, manual review, low adoption, delayed benefits, trust erosion, policy mistakes, remediation projects, relaunch efforts, and sometimes security or compliance exposure. Those costs are harder to forecast, harder to contain, and harder to defend.

A readiness investment usually improves economics in five ways.

First, it reduces avoidable rework. Fewer bad answers, fewer misrouted cases, fewer manual corrections, fewer duplicate investigations.

Second, it protects adoption. Employees will not keep using a system they do not trust. Trust is not an abstract benefit. It directly affects realized value.

Third, it shortens the path to stable operations. A disciplined launch may take longer than a rushed pilot, but it typically reaches dependable performance faster.

Fourth, it lowers hidden operating cost. Poorly governed AI tends to create recurring cleanup work that consumes support, content, security, and operations teams long after launch.

Fifth, it creates a reusable control pattern. The organization can extend the same readiness methods to other use cases rather than solving the same governance problems from scratch each time.

The management lesson is simple:

Getting data right looks more expensive on the plan.
Getting data wrong is usually more expensive in operations.

Exhibit 6E — Completed Example: Getting Data Right vs. Getting Data Wrong

The following figures are illustrative but calibrated to plausible enterprise operating conditions. Labor-rate assumptions are anchored to current U.S. Bureau of Labor Statistics wage data and employer compensation structure, then rounded for planning use.

Consider a mid-sized enterprise with **8,000 employees** that wants to launch a RAG-based assistant to answer internal questions on leave policies, travel rules, expense guidance, onboarding procedures, device ordering, and security requirements.

The organization handles about **28,800 policy-related inquiries per year**, or roughly **2,400 per month**. Average handling time is **9 minutes per inquiry**, with a loaded blended labor cost of **$38 per hour**. The relevant content exists, but it is spread across SharePoint sites, wikis, network folders, PDFs, and regional policy documents. The organization initially identifies **3,200 documents** in scope. Of these, about **24 percent** lack a clear owner and **30 percent** have no review date.

The organization faces two choices.

Path A — Get the data right before launch

In the governed path, the team begins with readiness work instead of rushing directly into deployment. It reduces the source set from **3,200 documents to 1,500 approved, in-scope documents**. It assigns owners to all policy domains, archives obsolete content, adds effective and review dates, applies metadata for geography, business unit, confidentiality, and document status, separates draft content from approved content, improves parsing for scanned PDFs and tables, enables permission-aware retrieval, requires citations in answers, and defines a fallback rule for conflicting or weakly supported answers.

The one-time readiness investment is estimated as:

- content inventory and cleanup: **$55,000**
- metadata and ownership assignment: **$30,000**
- parsing, chunking, and retrieval design: **$40,000**
- permission-aware indexing and controls: **$40,000**

- evaluation, citation testing, and fallback design: **$35,000**
- change management and rollout support: **$20,000**

That produces a **total one-time readiness cost of $220,000**.
Annual run cost is estimated at **$110,000**.

The baseline labor cost of handling **28,800 inquiries per year** at **9 minutes each** and **$38 per hour** is **$164,160 annually**.

After launch, the organization estimates that **50 percent** of routine inquiries are deflected to self-service, creating a direct savings of **$82,080**. It also expects the remaining inquiries to be handled **2 minutes faster**, creating an additional **$18,240** in labor savings. Reduced duplicate tickets and repeated follow-ups are estimated at **$42,000** per year. Faster onboarding and administrative coordination add **$55,000**, and avoided rework and escalations from conflicting policy answers add another **$48,000**.

That yields a **year-one quantified benefit of $245,320**.

Against **$330,000** in combined year-one readiness and run cost, the system produces a **net year-one result of -$84,680**.

That first-year result is not a weakness in the example. It is a strength. It reflects what many real enterprise knowledge initiatives look like: the first year pays for the foundation.

The three-year view is much stronger:

- **Year 1 benefit:** $245,320
- **Year 2 benefit:** $315,000
- **Year 3 benefit:** $315,000

Total 3-year benefit: $875,320

Against:

- **Year 1 cost:** $330,000
- **Year 2 cost:** $110,000
- **Year 3 cost:** $110,000

Total 3-year cost: $550,000

The result is a **net 3-year benefit of $325,320**, or a **3-year ROI of 59 percent**.

This is the economic logic of readiness. The organization is not merely buying a chatbot. It is building a trusted knowledge layer that becomes more valuable over time.

Path B — Launch before the data is ready

In the weak-governance path, the organization launches quickly. It performs no authoritative-source review, postpones ownership cleanup, accepts inconsistent metadata, mixes draft and approved content, applies only limited permission remediation, and relies on prompt tuning instead of disciplined retrieval design.

The rapid launch cost is estimated at **$95,000**, with annual run cost of **$110,000**.

Because trust is weaker and content quality is inconsistent, realized benefit is much lower. The organization captures only **$120,000** in benefit during year one.

At the same time, it incurs:

- manual review and correction burden: **$72,000**
- content cleanup and re-indexing: **$95,000**
- permission remediation and retesting: **$48,000**
- incident investigation and communications overhead: **$25,000**
- lost productivity from low adoption and duplicate checking: **$60,000**

That creates **$300,000 in additional failure and remediation cost**.

The year-one economics therefore become:

- **Total year-one cost:** $505,000
- **Total year-one benefit:** $120,000
- **Net year-one result: -$385,000**

This is the real comparison.

The governed path looks more expensive on the plan, but it creates a viable multi-year asset. The weak-readiness path looks cheaper at launch, but it becomes more expensive in operations and harder to trust.

That is the true economics of AI data readiness.

Exhibit 6F — Data Readiness Risk Register

A practical readiness review should identify the major risks that emerge when AI is placed into real workflows. The table below can be adapted for any use case, and especially for RAG-based enterprise assistants.

Risk 1 — Stale or obsolete content
What it looks like: the system retrieves old policies, superseded procedures, or outdated reference material.
Likely impact: wrong answers, user distrust, policy violations, rework.
Typical cause: no effective dates, no review cycle, weak archival discipline.
Control response: add review dates, ownership, freshness rules, and automatic exclusion of obsolete content.

Risk 2 — Conflicting source versions
What it looks like: the assistant cites two different answers to the same question.
Likely impact: confusion, escalations, leadership concern, failed adoption.
Typical cause: draft and approved content stored together; no authoritative-source rule.
Control response: define source precedence, separate drafts from approved material, and require fallback when conflicts remain unresolved.

Risk 3 — Permission leakage
What it looks like: users receive answers grounded in content they should not have access to.
Likely impact: security incident, privacy breach, regulatory exposure, trust damage.
Typical cause: retrieval layer not aligned to source permissions; weak access metadata.
Control response: enforce role-aware or user-aware retrieval, test boundary cases, and log retrieval events.

Risk 4 — Poor parsing or chunking quality
What it looks like: tables are broken, clauses are split incorrectly, or answers are grounded in incomplete fragments.
Likely impact: inaccurate or misleading answers despite apparently valid citations.
Typical cause: weak PDF extraction, poor chunking design, no testing on real document formats.
Control response: improve parsing, test chunk quality on representative documents, and evaluate retrieval accuracy before scale.

Risk 5 — Weak metadata discipline
What it looks like: the system cannot reliably filter by geography, business unit, policy type, confidentiality, or document status.
Likely impact: over-broad retrieval, wrong context, preventable policy errors.
Typical cause: missing metadata model or inconsistent tagging.
Control response: define mandatory metadata fields and enforce them at ingestion.

Risk 6 — No named content ownership
What it looks like: nobody knows who is responsible for keeping a source current or resolving contradictions.
Likely impact: slow remediation, stale content, recurring dispute over answers.
Typical cause: content accumulated over time without stewardship.
Control response: assign domain owners and make content review part of operational governance.

Risk 7 — No fallback under uncertainty
What it looks like: the assistant answers confidently even when evidence is weak, stale, or conflicting.
Likely impact: high-confidence wrong answers, reputational damage, unsafe scaling.
Typical cause: product design focused on answer rate instead of answer safety.
Control response: define confidence thresholds, abstention rules, and escalation paths.

Risk 8 — Retrieval poisoning or malicious source content
What it looks like: manipulated content influences outputs while appearing grounded.
Likely impact: security risk, misinformation, corrupted knowledge layer, hidden failure.
Typical cause: weak source controls, poor ingestion governance, insufficient security review.

Control response: restrict trusted sources, monitor change events, review sensitive corpora, and test adversarial scenarios.

Risk 9 — Hidden operating cost
What it looks like: teams spend ongoing effort correcting outputs, cleaning sources, and handling exceptions after launch.
Likely impact: eroded ROI, leadership frustration, stalled scale-out.
Typical cause: readiness work deferred until after deployment.
Control response: include readiness cost in the business case and treat it as a value-protection investment, not optional overhead.

How to Use This Register

This risk register should not sit in an appendix and be forgotten. It should be reviewed during business-case approval, readiness assessment, pilot exit, and production go-live review. It is most useful when each risk has a named owner, a current status, a target mitigation date, a residual risk rating, and an explicit go or no-go implication.

That discipline turns data readiness from a vague aspiration into a managed delivery condition.

Pilot Ready Is Not Production Ready

This distinction deserves explicit treatment because many AI teams blur it.

Pilot readiness means the team has enough structure to test feasibility.

Production readiness means the organization has enough discipline to trust the system at scale.

Pilot-ready environments often rely on curated content, manual review, expert supervision, and hidden cleanup work. Production-ready environments require repeatable ingestion, stable semantics, explicit ownership, permissions, monitoring, support processes, rollback paths, and a defensible control model.

If leaders do not distinguish the two, they will repeatedly approve pilots and then wonder why scale feels slower, more expensive, and more politically difficult than expected.

Red Flags

A use case is not ready when nobody can name the authoritative source, policy versions conflict without an owner, permissions will be "figured out later," citations are optional, a pilot depends on manual expert cleanup, the process is unstable but AI is expected to standardize it, there is no clear fallback when retrieval fails, stale content can remain indexed indefinitely, security has not assessed poisoning or injection risk, or nobody owns benefit realization and operational accountability together.

These are not minor technical issues. They are signs that trust has not been designed into the system.

Checklist Callout — Preconditions Before You Scale

Before scaling any AI use case, ask:

What exact workflow or decision is this system entering?
What source is authoritative?
What must be current, and how current?
Who owns the content and the business rule?
What exceptions exist?
What does the human reviewer control?
How is access enforced?
How are outputs traced and challenged?
What happens when the system is uncertain, conflicting, stale, or incomplete?
What monitoring proves that readiness still exists after go-live?

If these questions do not have clear answers, the project is not ready to scale.

Key Takeaway

AI success begins before the model.

It begins with whether the organization has created a trustworthy operating environment for the model to live in. That means data that is authoritative, accessible, current, traceable, governed, and continuously qualified. It also means workflows that are stable, owned, and explicit about where human control begins and ends.

RAG can be a powerful bridge from limited maturity to early enterprise value. But it is not a shortcut around discipline. It is a governed retrieval architecture that turns knowledge quality, permissions, freshness, parsing, chunking, retrieval evaluation, and citation integrity into first-class project concerns.

That is the real precondition for AI success.

References

Reviewed source evaluation:

1. N-iX, *Data readiness for AI: In-depth guide to effective AI performance* — strongest on use-case-specific readiness, governance, metadata, DataOps, unified access, and continuous qualification.
2. The Virtual Forge, *AI Data Readiness: How to Prepare Your Data for AI* — strongest on the distinction between custom training and RAG, and on the case for RAG as an early bridge with transparency and source traceability.
3. TELUS Digital, *How to Assess Data Readiness for AI: An Executive's Guide* — strongest on executive ownership, use-case prioritization, and a practical assessment sequence tied to business outcomes and targeted remediation.
4. Mia-Platform, *AI Data Readiness: Preparing Successful Data* — useful on context, accountability, metadata, lifecycle visibility, and continuous qualification, though the uploaded extraction is partially degraded in places.

Additional references:

5. NIST, *Artificial Intelligence Risk Management Framework: Generative Artificial Intelligence Profile* — useful for groundedness, provenance, and source and citation verification expectations.
6. AWS Prescriptive Guidance, *Data security, lifecycle, and strategy for generative AI applications* — useful for the point that RAG adds a distinct lifecycle and data pipeline of preparation, retrieval integration, evaluation, and ongoing updates.
7. AWS Prescriptive Guidance, *Retrieval-augmented generation options for question answering from custom documentation* — useful for the point that RAG references authoritative data sources outside model training data.
8. OWASP, *LLM Prompt Injection Prevention Cheat Sheet* — useful for retrieval poisoning and prompt-injection risk in RAG systems.
9. Microsoft Learn, *Retrieval Augmented Generation (RAG) in Azure AI Search* and related Azure guidance — useful for enterprise retrieval complexity, chunking, citations, multi-source access, and newer agentic retrieval patterns.

Chapter 7

Governance, Risk, and Control Design for AI Delivery

Once the organization has established that a use case is worth funding and that its data and workflow are sufficiently ready, a harder question appears:

How will this system actually be governed in production?

This is the chapter where many AI programs become serious.

Up to this point, an organization may still be speaking in the language of promise. It may be discussing value, readiness, architecture, and the conditions for success. All of that matters. But none of it is enough on its own. An AI system that is economically attractive and technically feasible can still fail because the organization never decided who had authority, which risks were acceptable, what controls were mandatory, when human review was required, how incidents would be handled, or what evidence would be retained to prove that the system remained trustworthy over time.

That is what governance is for.

Governance is not a slide about principles.
It is not a steering committee with no power.
It is not a legal memo attached late in the process.
It is not a one-time approval before launch.

Governance is the operating system for making AI decisions accountable.

A well-governed AI delivery model answers six practical questions before the system is trusted at scale:

Who owns the use case?
Who owns the risks?
Who decides what controls are required?
Who can approve release?
Who can stop the system?
Who is accountable when the system causes harm, drift, loss, or unacceptable behavior?

If those questions do not have clear answers, then the project is not governed. It is merely proceeding.

Current Signal — The Governance Direction Is Clear

The major frameworks are converging around a similar message even though their language differs. NIST's AI RMF is built around four functions — Govern, Map, Measure, and Manage — and treats AI risk as a lifecycle discipline rather than a one-time approval exercise. OECD's AI Principles promote trustworthy AI that respects human rights and democratic values, while OECD's accountability work explicitly links risk management to the AI lifecycle. ISO/IEC 42001 describes a structured AI management system for establishing, implementing, maintaining, and continually improving governance over AI. The European Commission's AI Act guidance is risk-based and sets staged applicability dates, with prohibited practices and AI literacy obligations applying from February 2, 2025, GPAI governance rules from August 2, 2025, and the Act becoming broadly applicable from August 2, 2026, with some exceptions. OWASP's current LLM guidance highlights concrete security failure modes such as prompt injection, insecure output handling, data poisoning, denial of service, and supply-chain vulnerabilities. (NIST Publications)

The strategic lesson is straightforward: governance is no longer optional polish. It is part of the delivery system. And because AI is still evolving quickly — in models, architectures, attack patterns, tooling, and regulatory expectations — organizations need governance that is durable enough to survive change rather than governance that depends on today's product fashion. (NIST Publications)

Governance Begins Before the Model Ships

A common mistake is to treat governance as a release checkpoint.

That is too late.

By the time an AI system is ready for go-live, many of the most important governance decisions have already been made, whether consciously or not. Someone has chosen the use case. Someone has selected the data. Someone has defined the success measure. Someone has decided whether human review remains mandatory or can be bypassed. Someone has chosen what the system can see, what it can say, what it can recommend, and what it can trigger. Someone has accepted the residual risk.

If those decisions are made informally, then informal governance is already in place. It is just weak governance.

That is why governance must begin early. It should shape:

- use-case selection

- risk tiering
- design choices
- data access
- human oversight model
- testing scope
- evidence requirements
- production release conditions
- monitoring and incident response

Governance is not the brake on AI delivery.

Poor governance is the brake. Good governance is what allows leadership to move faster with confidence because the rules, responsibilities, and stop conditions are already known.

Governance Is a Management System, Not a Meeting

Many organizations respond to AI risk by creating a committee. That may be necessary, but it is not sufficient.

A committee without decision rights is theater.
A policy without required controls is theater.
A review process without stage gates is theater.

Real governance means the organization has translated principles into mechanisms.

That usually includes:

- defined accountability
- risk classification
- mandatory controls by risk tier
- approval gates
- documentation requirements
- testing and validation standards

- exception management
- monitoring and incident response
- retraining, reapproval, or decommissioning triggers

A practical enterprise translation of the major frameworks is simple:

Governance should define who decides, what must be true before release, how risks are measured, and what happens when those conditions stop being true.

The Minimum Governance Questions

Before an AI system enters production, leadership should be able to answer:

What business decision or workflow is this system influencing?
What harm could occur if it is wrong, biased, manipulated, stale, or unavailable?
What level of autonomy does it have?
What human oversight is required?
What evidence supports release?
What would trigger rollback, suspension, or reapproval?

These are not legal questions alone. They are management questions.

If the organization cannot answer them clearly, the system is not ready for enterprise use.

Exhibit 7A — What AI Governance Must Actually Do

A working AI governance model should do five things.

First, assign authority.
It must define who owns the use case, the model or system behavior, the data inputs, the operational process, the risk posture, and the final approval to release.

Second, classify risk.
It must distinguish between low-risk assistive use cases and high-consequence systems that influence rights, access, money, safety, workforce decisions, regulated outcomes, or enterprise actions.

Third, require controls.
It must specify what controls are mandatory at each risk level: testing, human review,

logging, documentation, source controls, security review, explainability expectations, and fallback behavior.

Fourth, create release discipline.
It must define stage gates from design through pilot through production, including go/no-go conditions.

Fifth, sustain accountability after launch.
It must define monitoring, incident response, drift review, retraining or reindexing rules, audit evidence, and decommissioning triggers.

If governance does not do these five things, it is probably governance in name only.

The Governance Operating Model

An effective AI governance model usually distributes responsibility rather than centralizing everything in one body.

The business owner should remain accountable for the use case and realized value.
The delivery owner should remain accountable for implementation and controls.
Data owners should remain accountable for source quality, meaning, access, and readiness.
Security and privacy should assess risk and required safeguards.
Legal and compliance should interpret applicable obligations.
Operations should own post-launch performance, support, and escalation.
An AI review authority or board should resolve cross-functional issues, approve higher-risk releases, and enforce exceptions.

This structure matters because AI failures are often cross-functional. A hallucination may be a model problem, a retrieval problem, a content problem, a prompt problem, a permission problem, or an oversight problem. Governance fails when everyone assumes someone else owns the issue.

The model should therefore be explicit.

Exhibit 7B — Core Roles in the AI Governance Model

Business owner
Owns the use case, business objective, and value realization.

AI product or delivery owner
Owns end-to-end delivery, control implementation, and release readiness.

Data owner
Owns authority, semantics, access, freshness, and permitted use of data or knowledge sources.

Security and privacy leads
Own security review, access control expectations, data protection controls, and incident escalation.

Legal or compliance lead
Owns regulatory interpretation, policy alignment, records expectations, and required disclosures.

Operational owner
Owns post-launch support, monitoring, fallback handling, and performance review.

Human oversight owner
Owns named human review responsibilities where oversight is required by policy, risk, or law.

AI review authority
Owns final review of higher-risk cases, exceptions, and release conditions across functions.

The point is not bureaucracy. The point is that accountability must be named before the system scales.

Risk Tiering Is What Makes Governance Proportional

Not every AI use case needs the same level of control.

A low-risk drafting assistant does not need the same governance as an AI system that prioritizes vulnerable customers, influences employee decisions, approves benefits, or triggers production changes.

This is why risk tiering matters. The governance model should not force the same burden on every use case. It should scale controls in proportion to impact.

An internal enterprise risk tiering model might look like this:

Tier 1 — Assistive, low consequence
The system suggests, drafts, summarizes, or retrieves, but a human remains fully responsible before anything consequential happens.

Tier 2 — Operational influence
The system prioritizes, classifies, routes, or recommends within workflows where mistakes can create material cost, service, or compliance impact but can usually be intercepted.

Tier 3 — High consequence or regulated
The system materially influences rights, access, money, workforce decisions, public services, safety, or regulated outcomes, or it is embedded in critical operations with limited tolerance for failure.

The point of tiering is not classification for its own sake. It is to force appropriate controls.

Exhibit 7C — Illustrative Control Expectations by Risk Tier

Tier 1
Requires source controls, basic testing, usage policy, human review, logging, and monitored feedback.

Tier 2
Requires all Tier 1 controls plus defined fallback paths, stronger evaluation, documented oversight, security review, role clarity, incident thresholds, and release approval beyond the project team.

Tier 3
Requires all Tier 2 controls plus formal risk assessment, deeper validation, explicit human oversight design, stronger audit evidence, tighter change control, executive accountability, and formal stop conditions.

This is where governance becomes useful. It matches control cost to consequence.

Human Oversight Must Be Designed, Not Assumed

One of the weakest phrases in AI programs is "human in the loop."

It sounds reassuring, but it often hides ambiguity.

Which human?
At what point?
With what authority?
Reviewing what evidence?
Able to override what behavior?

Within what time window?
With what training?

That is why governance needs more than a slogan. It needs an oversight design.

Current public guidance under the EU AI Act makes the point clearly for relevant settings: deployers must assign human oversight to persons who are sufficiently equipped and enabled to exercise it meaningfully. (Digital Strategy EU)

For enterprise governance, the practical lesson is broader than legal compliance:

Human oversight is only real if the person has authority, context, training, and time to intervene meaningfully.

Anything less is symbolic oversight.

Control Design Must Reach Into the System

A governance charter alone will not protect the enterprise unless it is translated into system behavior.

Control design should reach into:

- access permissions
- source allow-lists
- confidence thresholds
- abstain-or-escalate rules
- action limits
- approval rules
- logging
- monitoring
- change control
- incident handling

This is especially true for generative AI and RAG-based systems. Current security guidance emphasizes that risks can emerge not only from prompts, but from insecure outputs, poisoned data, denial-of-service patterns, and supply-chain weakness. (OWASP Foundation)

That means governance cannot stop at policy statements. It must show up in:

- what the system is allowed to access
- what outputs are blocked or escalated
- how external content is trusted or rejected
- what evidence is retained
- when the system must stop or degrade safely

Good governance is visible in runtime behavior.

Stage Gates Matter More Than Good Intentions

Most organizations already have project stage gates for capital, security, architecture, or release management. AI should not sit outside that discipline.

It should usually have its own delivery gates, because AI introduces risks that ordinary software governance does not fully cover: model uncertainty, data drift, retrieval quality, oversight design, explainability, prompt injection, bias, content conflict, and dynamic behavior over time.

A practical AI stage-gate sequence often includes:

Gate 1 — Use-case approval
Is the use case legitimate, valuable, and within policy?

Gate 2 — Readiness approval
Are the data, workflow, and ownership conditions strong enough to proceed?

Gate 3 — Control design approval
Have the required controls been identified and built into the design?

Gate 4 — Pilot release approval
Is the pilot sufficiently bounded, monitored, and reversible?

Gate 5 — Production release approval
Has the system produced enough evidence to justify scaled use?

Gate 6 — Ongoing review
Does post-launch evidence still support continued operation?

This is not over-engineering. It is the governance equivalent of responsible release management.

Exhibit 7D — AI Delivery Stage-Gate Questions

At each gate, the review should ask a disciplined set of questions.

For **use-case approval**:
What business objective is being served?
What could go wrong?
What risk tier applies?
Who owns the business outcome?

For **readiness approval**:
Are the data and workflow ready enough?
Are authoritative sources and permissions defined?
Is human oversight designed?

For **control design approval**:
What controls are mandatory for this tier?
How will the system abstain, escalate, or fail safely?
What evidence will be retained?

For **pilot approval**:
Is the pilot bounded by scope, user group, and rollback conditions?
What will be measured?
What would cause pilot suspension?

For **production approval**:
What evidence proves the system is stable, reliable, and governable?
Who signs off?
What incident thresholds trigger rollback?

For **ongoing review**:
What has changed since release?
What drift, incidents, or user behavior signal new risk?
Does the system still deserve to operate as approved?

These questions turn governance into a living discipline instead of a one-time checkpoint.

Documentation Is Not Bureaucracy. It Is Evidence

A governance model that produces no evidence produces little trust.

Documentation should be right-sized, but it should exist. At minimum, higher-value or higher-risk AI systems should have:

- use-case summary
- risk tier determination
- data and source description
- oversight design
- testing summary
- security and privacy review outcome
- release decision record
- change log
- incident log
- periodic review record

The point is not to create binders.

The point is to make decisions traceable.

AI Literacy Is a Governance Requirement

Many governance failures are not caused by lack of policy. They are caused by lack of understanding.

People sign off on systems they do not understand.
Managers rely on outputs they cannot challenge.
Reviewers assume human oversight exists when it does not.
Teams over trust fluent systems because they sound confident.

This is why AI literacy belongs inside governance, not beside it.

The EU AI Act's literacy provisions took effect on February 2, 2025, alongside the rules on prohibited practices. (Digital Strategy EU)

For enterprise practice, that means training should not be generic awareness only. It should be role-based. Executives, approvers, frontline reviewers, technical teams, and support teams each need different competence.

A governance model that assumes understanding without building it is a fragile model.

Incident Response Must Exist Before the First Incident

AI incidents are not hypothetical.

Even well-designed systems can produce harmful or unacceptable outcomes because sources change, usage changes, edge cases appear, or adversarial behavior emerges. Current security guidance for LLM applications exists precisely because these risks are now recurring and practical, not theoretical. (OWASP Foundation)

That means governance should define, before launch:

- what counts as an incident
- severity levels
- who must be notified
- what evidence must be preserved
- when the system must be disabled, degraded, or rolled back
- how root cause analysis is conducted
- who approves return to service

Without this, incident response becomes improvisation under pressure.

And in AI, improvisation tends to erode trust faster than the original technical issue.

Exhibit 7E — Completed Example: Governance Design for AI-Assisted Ticket Triage

Consider the use case introduced earlier: AI-assisted ticket triage and routing for an enterprise support organization.

The system classifies tickets, recommends urgency and impact, routes tickets to resolver groups, and drafts a short summary for the receiving analyst.

This sounds operationally useful and relatively safe. But governance still matters because the system can affect SLA performance, customer experience, workload distribution, escalation speed, and downstream reporting.

The organization assigns it **Tier 2 — Operational influence**.

The governance design includes the following:

Business owner
Director of Service Operations

Delivery owner
AI Product Manager for Support Automation

Data owner
Service Management Platform Owner

Security and privacy review
Required before pilot because tickets may contain sensitive information

Human oversight model
During pilot, all routing remains overridable by service desk leads.
After production release, automated routing is allowed only within defined confidence and policy boundaries; exceptions are sent to human triage.

Required controls

- approved ticket taxonomy
- authoritative routing rules
- logging of model recommendation and final routed group
- confidence threshold for automation
- override capture and reason codes
- monthly error review
- incident escalation if misrouting crosses agreed threshold

- rollback path to rules-only routing

Pilot gate conditions

- baseline misroute rate established
- taxonomy cleanup completed
- routing recommendations tested on representative historical tickets
- override interface available
- audit log confirmed
- support leads trained on oversight role

Production gate conditions

- pilot misroute improvement demonstrated
- no unresolved security issue
- override and escalation procedures tested
- business owner accepts residual risk
- operations team accepts monitoring burden

Ongoing review

- monthly misroute rate
- high-priority ticket error review
- override trend analysis
- taxonomy change review
- retraining or recalibration trigger if performance deteriorates

This is governance in practical form. It is not abstract. It defines authority, controls, stage gates, oversight, metrics, and stop conditions.

Governance Must Cover Change, Not Just Launch

A common governance failure is to treat launch approval as the finish line.

In AI, it is only the start of accountable operation.

Models are updated. Prompts are modified. Source content changes. Retrieval logic changes. Thresholds are tuned. Users discover new behaviors. Systems are connected to new tools. Context shifts.

Every one of those changes can alter risk.

That is why change control matters. Significant changes should trigger one or more of the following:

- retesting
- review of affected controls
- reapproval by the relevant authority
- updated documentation
- targeted communications or retraining
- rollback planning

The principle is simple:

No material AI change should enter production without governance asking whether the approved risk posture still holds.

Governance Should Also Know How Systems End

Organizations often plan AI launches with enthusiasm and decommissioning with neglect.

But systems may need to be retired because value did not materialize, risks increased, regulation changed, better approaches replaced them, or supporting data and workflows no longer remain trustworthy.

NIST's AI RMF treats decommissioning and other end-of-life processes as part of responsible governance across the lifecycle. (NIST Publications)

That is a valuable reminder. Governance is not complete unless it includes the end of life.

Systems should be retired with the same discipline used to release them:

- defined trigger for retirement
- archival of required records
- communication to users
- rollback or replacement planning
- removal of unnecessary access and integrations

A system that no longer deserves to operate should not remain in production by inertia.

Red Flags

Governance is probably weak when:

- no one can name the final accountable business owner
- risk tiering is absent or symbolic
- human oversight is described but not designed
- the project team can release without independent challenge
- controls are discussed but not embedded in system behavior
- exception handling depends on heroic individuals
- there is no rollback plan
- incident handling is undefined
- documentation is scattered or missing
- retraining, reindexing, or major prompt changes bypass review
- literacy is assumed rather than built

These are not cosmetic issues. They are signs that the organization is asking trust to exist without building the machinery that makes trust durable.

The Economics of Governance

Good governance is often resisted because its costs are visible early.

The organization sees policy work, role definition, control design, logging, stage gates, review time, testing, training, and monitoring. It sees meetings, documents, and implementation effort. Those costs are real.

But poor governance does not remove cost. It relocates cost.

Instead of paying in planned control design, the organization pays later in rework, incidents, manual checking, remediation, delayed adoption, stalled scale, and sometimes legal or contractual exposure. The cost is often larger because the system has already been launched, users have already lost confidence, and technical debt has already accumulated.

This is where governance becomes a business decision rather than a philosophy discussion.

Environmental Scan — What the Literature Suggests About Cost and Value

The authoritative literature does not offer one universal formula for AI governance ROI. But it does converge on a clear structure. NIST frames risk management as the comparison between current and target profiles, including the staffing and funding needed to reach target outcomes in a cost-effective way. OECD's accountability work links lifecycle risk management to trustworthy AI and emphasizes mechanisms to define, assess, treat, and govern risks throughout the lifecycle. ISO/IEC 42001 presents AI governance as a management system with continual improvement rather than ad hoc control. Together, these sources support treating governance as a value-protection and loss-reduction investment, not merely a compliance overhead. (NIST Publications)

That leads to a practical enterprise method:

- define the use case and risk tier
- describe the poor-governance current state
- describe the good-governance target state
- identify major governance-related loss scenarios
- estimate expected annual loss under both states
- estimate one-time and annual governance cost
- compare avoided loss, improved value realization, and governance spend

That method is simple enough to use in real portfolio decisions and disciplined enough to make governance visible in economic terms.

Exhibit 7F — Methodology for Comparing Poor AI Governance vs. Good AI Governance

A practical governance analysis should compare two operating states:

State 1 — Poor governance
The AI system is launched with partial ownership, weak controls, limited monitoring, and unclear oversight.

State 2 — Good governance
The AI system is launched with named accountability, risk-tiered controls, release gates, logging, human oversight, monitoring, and incident response.

The analysis should proceed in six steps:

1. Define the use case and risk tier.
2. Build a current poor-governance profile and a target good-governance profile.
3. Identify governance-related risk scenarios.
4. Estimate expected annual loss for each scenario under both profiles.
5. Estimate one-time and annual governance cost.
6. Compare avoided loss, improved value realization, and governance investment.

This method does not require false precision. It requires disciplined estimation, named assumptions, and consistent comparison.

Exhibit 7G — Governance Risk Categories and Cost Logic

Poor AI governance tends to create cost in five main ways.

First, it raises failure frequency.
Without clear controls, more things go wrong more often.

Second, it raises failure severity.
Without logging, oversight, and incident triggers, small problems become larger and more expensive.

Third, it delays detection.
Weak monitoring means issues persist longer before action is taken.

Fourth, it lowers trust and adoption.
Users compensate by checking outputs manually or abandoning the system.

Fifth, it delays scale.
Leadership becomes reluctant to extend the AI use case into new workflows.

Good governance changes those economics by lowering the probability of failure, reducing the severity of incidents, accelerating detection, protecting trust, and increasing the percentage of projected business value that is actually realized.

Exhibit 7H — Completed Example: AI Ticket Triage Under Poor Governance vs. Good Governance

The following figures are illustrative but calibrated to plausible enterprise operating conditions. Labor-rate assumptions are anchored to current U.S. Bureau of Labor Statistics wage data and employer compensation structure, then rounded for planning use.

To make the economics of governance concrete, return to the ticket-triage use case from Chapter 5.

The support organization estimates that, if the system is trusted and broadly adopted, the use case has a **potential annual gross value of $576,000**. That is the steady-state benefit identified in the business case. The governance question is not whether the use case has value in theory. The governance question is how much of that value will actually be realized under weak versus strong control conditions, and how much loss will occur along the way.

Summary table

Metric	Poor Governance	Good Governance	Difference
Potential annual gross value	$576,000	$576,000	—
One-time setup cost	$160,000	$285,000	+$125,000
Annual run cost	$85,000	$120,000	+$35,000
Expected annual loss	$310,000	$95,000	**-$215,000**
Realized annual value	$288,000	$490,000	**+$202,000**
Value realization rate	50%	85%	+35 pts
Expected net annual value	**-$107,000**	**$275,000**	**+$382,000**

Good governance raises upfront and run cost, but materially lowers expected loss, improves realized value, and turns the use case from negative to positive annual expected value.

Scenario A — Poor governance

In the weak-governance scenario, the organization launches quickly. It has no formal risk tiering, weak confidence thresholds, limited logging, unclear override responsibility, no structured incident review, and no periodic recalibration review.

One-time setup cost is **$160,000**.
Annual run cost is **$85,000**.

Because governance is weak, expected annual loss is higher:

- operational rework and bad routing: **$110,000**
- SLA and customer impact: **$70,000**
- security, privacy, and control failures: **$35,000**
- incident remediation and retesting: **$55,000**
- trust erosion and manual checking burden: **$40,000**

That produces a **total expected annual loss of $310,000**.

Because the system is less trusted and requires more human checking, the organization realizes only **50 percent** of potential value, or **$288,000** annually.

The resulting expected annual value is:

- realized benefit: **$288,000**
- less annual run cost: **$85,000**
- less expected annual loss: **$310,000**

Expected net annual value: -$107,000

The use case looked cheaper to launch. It became uneconomic to operate.

Scenario B — Good governance

In the strong-governance scenario, the organization applies a **Tier 2 risk classification**, names a business owner and operational owner, establishes confidence thresholds for automated routing, requires override capture, logs recommendations and final actions, uses pilot and production release gates, conducts monthly quality review, defines rollback triggers, and trains human oversight leads.

One-time setup and governance cost is **$285,000**.
Annual run cost is **$120,000**.

Expected annual loss falls substantially:

- operational rework and bad routing: **$35,000**
- SLA and customer impact: **$20,000**
- security, privacy, and control failures: **$10,000**
- incident remediation and retesting: **$15,000**
- trust erosion and manual checking burden: **$15,000**

That produces a **total expected annual loss of $95,000**.

Because the system is more trusted and better governed, the organization realizes **85 percent** of the use case's potential value, or **$490,000** annually.

The resulting expected annual value is:

- realized benefit: **$490,000**
- less annual run cost: **$120,000**
- less expected annual loss: **$95,000**

Expected net annual value: $275,000

The lesson is clear:

Good governance costs more to design.
Poor governance costs more to live with.

In this example, stronger governance converts the use case from negative expected value to strongly positive expected value.

A common governance failure is to treat launch approval as the finish line.

In AI, it is only the start of accountable operation.

Models are updated. Prompts are modified. Source content changes. Retrieval logic changes. Thresholds are tuned. Users discover new behaviors. Systems are connected to new tools. Context shifts.

Every one of those changes can alter risk.

That is why change control matters. Significant changes should trigger one or more of the following:

- retesting
- review of affected controls
- reapproval by the relevant authority
- updated documentation
- targeted communications or retraining
- rollback planning

The principle is simple:

No material AI change should enter production without governance asking whether the approved risk posture still holds.

Governance Should Also Know How Systems End

Organizations often plan AI launches with enthusiasm and decommissioning with neglect.

But systems may need to be retired because value did not materialize, risks increased, regulation changed, better approaches replaced them, or supporting data and workflows no longer remain trustworthy.

That is a valuable reminder. Governance is not complete unless it includes the end of life.

Systems should be retired with the same discipline used to release them:

- defined trigger for retirement
- archival of required records
- communication to users
- rollback or replacement planning
- removal of unnecessary access and integrations

A system that no longer deserves to operate should not remain in production by inertia.

Checklist Callout — Before You Approve AI Governance for Delivery

Before approving a system for scaled use, ask:

Who owns the business outcome?
Who owns the risks?
What risk tier applies?
What controls are mandatory for that tier?
What human oversight exists in real operating terms?
What evidence supports release?
What incidents require suspension or rollback?
Who can authorize exceptions?
What changes require reapproval?
How will the system be monitored, reviewed, and eventually retired?

If these questions are not answered clearly, governance is not complete.

Key Takeaway

AI governance is not a side activity. It is the enterprise mechanism that turns AI from experimentation into accountable delivery.

It works when authority is named, risk is tiered, controls are mandatory, oversight is real, evidence is retained, incidents are managed, and change is governed after launch as rigorously as design was governed before it.

Without that, AI programs may still launch. They just will not scale with confidence.

With it, the organization gains something more valuable than approval.

It gains controlled permission to move.

References

1. NIST, *Artificial Intelligence Risk Management Framework (AI RMF 1.0)* — source for the Govern, Map, Measure, and Manage functions; lifecycle governance; current-versus-target profile logic; and decommissioning as part of governance. (NIST Publications)

2. NIST, *Artificial Intelligence Risk Management Framework: Generative AI Profile* — source for current lifecycle-oriented risk management guidance specific to generative AI. (NIST Publications)

3. OECD, *AI Principles* — source for trustworthy AI that respects human rights and democratic values. (OECD)

4. OECD, *Advancing Accountability in AI* — source for integrating risk management and the AI lifecycle to define, assess, treat, and govern risks throughout the lifecycle. (OECD)

5. ISO, *ISO/IEC 42001:2023 — AI management systems* — source for a structured AI management system with continual improvement and governance over risks and opportunities. (ISO)

6. European Commission, *AI Act | Shaping Europe's digital future* — source for the AI Act's timeline, risk-based structure, and staged applicability. (Digital Strategy EU)

7. European Commission, *Navigating the AI Act* — source for current public guidance on oversight, lifecycle duties, and implementation detail. (Digital Strategy EU)

8. OWASP, *Top 10 for Large Language Model Applications* — source for prompt injection, insecure output handling, training data poisoning, denial of service, and supply-chain vulnerabilities in LLM applications. (OWASP Foundation)

Chapter 8

Validation, Testing, and Evidence: How AI Earns the Right to Scale

An AI system should not scale because a demo impressed people.

It should scale because the organization has enough evidence to trust it.

That is the difference between experimentation and enterprise delivery.

By the time a project reaches this chapter, the use case has been chosen, the business case has been made, the data and workflow have been assessed, and the governance model has been defined. But one question still stands between a promising pilot and broader deployment:

What proof does the organization have that this system works well enough, safely enough, and reliably enough in the conditions that matter?

That is the purpose of validation, testing, and evidence.

In current authoritative guidance, this is not treated as optional polish. NIST's AI RMF explicitly highlights the importance of test, evaluation, verification, and validation — TEVV — throughout the AI lifecycle, and says these processes should be objective, repeatable or scalable, documented, and used for both mid-course remediation and post-hoc risk management. NIST also places TEVV actors across the lifecycle and separates those building models from those verifying and validating them as a best practice.

This chapter is where AI earns the right to scale.

Validation Is Not Just a Technical Exercise

One of the biggest mistakes in AI delivery is to treat testing as a job for technical specialists alone.

Engineers, data scientists, ML engineers, platform teams, and security teams all play essential roles. They design experiments. They tune models. They build evaluation harnesses. They measure latency, failure, accuracy, robustness, and drift. They are indispensable.

But enterprise validation is broader than that.

The organization also has to decide:

- what must be proven before release
- what evidence is good enough
- which scenarios matter most
- which risks are unacceptable
- which metrics count as release blockers
- what must be monitored after go-live
- who signs off on the evidence
- when the evidence no longer supports continued scale

Those are not purely technical decisions. They are delivery, governance, and business decisions.

This is where the **AI Project Manager** becomes distinct from technical resources. The technical team proves whether the system *can* perform. The AI Project Manager ensures the organization knows **what must be proven, by whom, by when, against which criteria, with which evidence, and for which gate decision**. The AI Project Manager is the orchestrator of the evidence program. The technical team generates much of the proof; the AI Project Manager makes that proof decision-ready. This role distinction is fully consistent with NIST's lifecycle view, where multiple AI actors contribute to TEVV and governance decisions across design, deployment, operation, and monitoring.

That distinction matters because many AI projects do not fail for lack of tests. They fail because tests were fragmented, poorly scoped, disconnected from real risk, or not translated into release evidence that leaders could rely on.

Testing, Validation, and Evidence Are Not the Same Thing

These terms are often used interchangeably. They should not be.

Testing asks whether the system behaves in a defined way under defined conditions. **Validation** asks whether the system is fit for its intended purpose in its real context of use. **Evidence** is the documented body of proof used to support go/no-go, scale, rollback, or redesign decisions.

A model can test well in the lab and still fail validation in the business.
A system can pass technical checks and still lack sufficient evidence for scale.
A pilot can produce promising anecdotes and still not justify deployment.

NIST's Generative AI Profile makes this point clearly. It warns that current pre-deployment testing approaches for generative AI can be inadequate, inconsistently applied, or mismatched to deployment contexts, and that benchmark-style testing or anecdotal demonstrations do not guarantee validity or reliability in real domains. It also notes that gaps between laboratory and real-world settings are especially serious for generative AI because of prompt sensitivity and the wide variation in contexts of use.

That is why a serious AI program needs all three:

- technical testing
- contextual validation
- a documented evidence pack for decision-makers

Exhibit 8A — What Each Term Means

Testing
Measures system behavior under planned conditions. Examples include accuracy tests, retrieval tests, safety tests, latency tests, red-team exercises, prompt-injection tests, and regression tests.

Validation
Determines whether the system is appropriate for the real use case, user group, workflow, and consequence level. Examples include pilot outcomes, structured field testing, fairness assessment, human-oversight performance, and outcome review in production-like conditions.

Evidence
The documented body of proof used to support governance and release decisions. Examples include evaluation results, known limitations, issue logs, override rates, incident results, benchmark summaries, field-test findings, sign-off records, and monitoring thresholds.

If an organization confuses these three, it will often overstate readiness.

What Good Validation Has to Prove

An enterprise AI system does not need to prove perfection. It needs to prove controlled fitness for purpose.

That means validation should answer questions such as:

- Does the system perform acceptably on the tasks it was approved for?
- Does it fail safely when confidence is weak or evidence is conflicting?
- Does it behave acceptably across the user groups, content types, and conditions it will actually face?
- Can humans meaningfully oversee it?
- Are the outputs explainable enough for the context?
- Are the security, privacy, and integrity risks within tolerance?
- Does the system continue to perform under real usage, not just in curated tests?

NIST's AI RMF treats these issues as part of trustworthiness and MEASURE activities, including validity, reliability, safety, and documented limitations. The GAI Profile adds specific actions such as comparing outputs to known ground truth, using both human oversight and automated evaluation, fact-checking generated information, evaluating performance in real-world scenarios, monitoring override behavior, and using staged release where needed.

The implication is simple: validation is not just "does it answer correctly?" It is "does it deserve to operate under these conditions?"

The Limits of Benchmark Thinking

A large share of AI testing failure comes from overreliance on narrow benchmarks.

Benchmark scores are useful. They are not enough.

A model may perform well on internal test prompts and still fail under realistic workload, ambiguous user behavior, poor source quality, domain-specific edge cases, conflicting instructions, or adversarial attempts. NIST explicitly warns that current pre-deployment TEVV for GAI may remain too focused on laboratory conditions or restricted benchmark datasets and may not extrapolate well to real deployment conditions. It also warns that tests designed for humans or anecdotal demonstrations do not guarantee system validity or reliability in domain use.

That means the enterprise should stop asking, “What was the benchmark score?” as if that settles the question.

A better question is, “What evidence do we have that this system performs acceptably in the real settings we are about to expose it to?”

Validation Must Include Real-World Use

This is especially important for GenAI, copilots, and RAG-based systems.

NIST’s GAI Profile recommends evaluating GAI system performance in real-world scenarios to reveal issues that do not surface in optimized testing environments. It also highlights structured public feedback, field testing, and AI red-teaming as ways to calibrate and verify traditional measurement methods. Field testing, in NIST’s description, is used to simulate deployment conditions and assess how people interact with and act on AI-generated content.

That is a major management point.

The goal is not merely to test the model in isolation. The goal is to validate the **human-AI configuration**: the prompts, the retrieval layer, the workflow, the approval steps, the user behavior, the override design, the escalation path, and the downstream consequences of being wrong.

This is why pilots matter — but only if they are instrumented as validation exercises rather than treated as enthusiasm campaigns.

Security Testing Is Part of Validation

A system that performs well functionally but is easy to manipulate is not ready to scale.

Current OWASP guidance for LLM applications identifies prompt injection, insecure output handling, training data poisoning, model denial of service, supply-chain vulnerabilities, sensitive information disclosure, and insecure plugin design as major classes of risk. These are not separate from validation. They are part of validating whether the system can safely operate in the environment it will enter.

For AI systems, especially those using external tools, enterprise data, or retrieval, the validation plan should usually include:

- prompt-injection resistance testing

- malicious-content and poisoning scenarios
- insecure-output and downstream-action testing
- access-boundary testing
- denial-of-service and excessive-cost scenarios
- third-party dependency review
- sensitive-data leakage tests

If these are omitted, the organization may end up validating usefulness while ignoring exploitability.

Exhibit 8B — Core Validation Domains

A complete validation program should usually cover six domains.

1. Functional performance
Does the system perform the task well enough on representative inputs?

2. Trustworthiness and safety
Does it remain valid, reliable, safe, and explainable enough for the context?

3. Security and resilience
Can it withstand injection, poisoning, abuse, leakage, excessive cost, and misuse?

4. Human oversight effectiveness
Do reviewers catch what they need to catch, and do they have usable evidence to intervene?

5. Operational fit
Does the system work under realistic load, latency, source freshness, and workflow conditions?

6. Monitoring readiness
Can the organization detect degradation, drift, overrides, incidents, and loss of value after launch?

If one of these domains is missing, the validation story is incomplete.

What the Evidence Pack Should Contain

An AI system should not move into production with only scattered test notes and a thumbs-up from the technical team.

The evidence should be assembled in a structured form so governance and business leaders can see what has been proven, what has not, and where the residual risk remains.

A practical evidence pack should usually include:

- use-case statement and approved scope
- risk tier and required controls
- test plan and validation criteria
- representative scenarios and datasets used
- results summary by test domain
- known limitations and excluded conditions
- security findings and mitigations
- human-oversight design and results
- field-test or pilot findings
- release recommendation
- open issues, waivers, and decision log
- post-launch monitoring plan

This is where ISO/IEC 42001 is especially useful conceptually. It frames AI management as a system of policies, objectives, processes, monitoring, and continual improvement rather than isolated technical checks. That is exactly the mindset the evidence pack should support.

The evidence pack is not bureaucracy. It is the artifact that allows the organization to say, with discipline, "Here is why this system deserves the next level of deployment."

The AI Project Manager's Role

This chapter is where the AI Project Manager becomes visible in a distinctive way.

The AI Project Manager is not the primary model builder. Not the main evaluator. Not the security tester. Not the lead data scientist.

But the AI Project Manager is the person who must ensure that the validation effort becomes a managed delivery stream rather than a pile of disconnected technical activities.

That means the AI Project Manager should typically own or orchestrate:

- validation planning and calendar alignment
- evidence requirements by stage gate
- coordination across technical, domain, risk, and operations teams
- traceability from risks to tests to findings to decisions
- entry and exit criteria for pilot and production gates
- issue escalation and decision logging
- residual-risk documentation
- readiness communication to sponsors and governance bodies
- monitoring handoff into operations

The technical teams produce much of the proof. The AI Project Manager turns that proof into **release evidence**.

Without that role, organizations often fall into one of two failure modes:

- the technical team tests a lot, but the project cannot answer governance questions clearly
- the governance body asks for evidence late, and the project scrambles to reconstruct it after the fact

Neither is a sign of maturity.

Exhibit 8C — AI Project Manager vs. AI Technical Resources in Validation

AI technical resources are primarily responsible for:

- designing and running experiments
- building test harnesses

- tuning models and prompts
- measuring technical performance
- executing security and robustness tests
- analyzing failure patterns
- implementing fixes

The AI Project Manager is primarily responsible for:

- defining what evidence is required for each gate
- aligning test scope to business and governance risk
- coordinating domain experts, evaluators, security, and operations
- ensuring representative scenarios are covered
- tracking findings, blockers, waivers, and residual risks
- assembling the evidence pack
- making the release decision process auditable and decision-ready

The difference is important.

Technical teams answer, "What did the system do?"
The AI Project Manager helps the organization answer, "Is that proof sufficient to proceed?"

Stage-Gated Validation

Validation should not wait until the end.

It should be staged.

Early stages should test basic feasibility, harmful failure modes, and scope discipline.
Pilot stages should test workflow fit, user behavior, override design, and realistic failure handling.
Pre-production stages should test release readiness, monitoring readiness, and rollback conditions.
Post-launch stages should test whether the real-world evidence still supports continued operation.

NIST's GAI Profile supports this view by recommending iterative TEVV, sharing pre-deployment results with release approval authorities, using real-world evaluation, and considering staged release approaches in light of projected use cases and organizational risk tolerance.

This makes validation a lifecycle discipline rather than a final hurdle.

What Good Exit Criteria Look Like

A pilot should not "pass" because stakeholders liked it.

It should pass because specific exit criteria were met.

Good exit criteria are usually:

- tied to the use case
- tied to the risk tier
- measurable
- linked to known limitations
- reviewed by the right decision-makers

Examples:

- routing accuracy exceeds threshold on representative cases
- override rate remains below agreed level
- harmful or unsupported outputs remain below tolerance
- security tests show no critical unresolved issue
- retrieval citations remain grounded above threshold
- human reviewers correctly intervene in defined scenarios
- latency and uptime remain within the approved operating envelope

The AI Project Manager should ensure these criteria exist before pilot begins, not after the results arrive.

Overrides, Incidents, and User Friction Are Evidence Too

Another common mistake is to treat only benchmark metrics as evidence.

In real deployment, some of the most important evidence comes from:

- how often humans override the system
- what kinds of cases trigger override
- where users stop trusting the output
- how often the system abstains
- which content types fail most often
- how often the workflow bypasses the AI because it is slower or less trusted
- what incidents or near misses occur

NIST's GAI Profile specifically recommends monitoring and documenting instances where humans override GAI decisions and evaluating those cases. It also recommends involving end-users, practitioners, and operators in prototyping and testing, including crisis scenarios.

That is a powerful reminder:

User friction is not noise. It is evidence.

Completed Example — Validation and Evidence for AI-Assisted Ticket Triage

Consider again the AI-assisted ticket-triage use case.

The system classifies tickets, recommends urgency and impact, routes tickets to resolver groups, and drafts a short summary for the receiving analyst. The delivery question in this chapter is not whether the model can produce plausible outputs. It is whether the organization has enough evidence to justify limited scale.

The use case handles **240,000 tickets per year** in production and is classified as **Tier 2 — Operational influence**.

The validation program is designed in three parts.

1. Historical validation set

A validation set of **24,000 tickets** is drawn from the previous 12 months. It is balanced to include routine incidents, service requests, high-priority incidents, known difficult routing cases, and ambiguous or incomplete tickets. A human-reviewed "gold label" route is assigned for evaluation purposes.

2. Controlled pilot

The organization runs an **8-week pilot** involving **16 service desk leads and senior triage agents**. The pilot covers **14,500 live tickets**. The AI recommends urgency, impact, route, and summary. Humans retain full override authority on all pilot tickets.

3. Security and resilience testing

The validation program also includes **250 adversarial or malformed ticket descriptions**, including injection-style language, attempts to force incorrect urgency escalation, and attempts to produce misleading summaries.

Exit criteria defined before the pilot

Validation metric	Threshold	Pilot result	Status
Correct resolver-group recommendation	≥ 78%	82%	Pass
High-priority ticket recall	≥ 95%	96.4%	Pass
Harmful misroute rate on high-priority tickets	≤ 2.0%	1.1%	Pass
Human override rate after week 4	≤ 20%	17.8%	Pass
Median response latency	≤ 2.5 sec	1.6 sec	Pass
Critical security findings unresolved	0	0	Pass
Summary usefulness rating from triage leads	≥ 4.0/5	4.2/5	Pass

Evidence generated during validation

Historical testing estimates a manual baseline correct-routing rate of about **65 percent**. AI recommendation accuracy on the validation set reaches **82 percent**, representing a **17-point improvement**.

During the live pilot:

- tickets processed: **14,500**
- overrides: **2,581**
- override rate: **17.8%**

The override causes are also analyzed:

- incomplete user description: **31%**
- conflicting category signals: **24%**
- business-rule exception: **19%**
- recent team ownership change not reflected in routing logic: **14%**
- other: **12%**

Operationally, average triage handling time falls from **4.8 minutes to 3.5 minutes** during the pilot. That is a savings of **1.3 minutes per ticket**. Across **14,500 pilot tickets**, that produces:

- **314 hours saved**
- at **$41/hour**, approximately **$12,874** in pilot labor savings

That pilot savings number is deliberately modest. It reflects a realistic validation mindset: the pilot's primary job is not to produce dramatic savings headlines. Its job is to generate evidence.

Validation conclusion

The pilot does **not** prove that unrestricted autonomy is safe.

It **does** prove that:

- routing assistance is materially better than baseline
- high-priority handling remains within tolerance
- human oversight catches important exceptions
- no critical unresolved security issue blocks-controlled production
- the evidence is strong enough for a **limited production release**

Release decision

The approved next step is a controlled production rollout to approved resolver groups, with:

- automated routing only above defined confidence thresholds
- mandatory logging of recommendations and final actions
- monthly override review
- rollback if harmful misroute rate exceeds **2 percent** for two consecutive review periods

This is what validation should look like in an enterprise setting.

The data scientist, engineers, and security specialists generate much of the proof.
The **AI Project Manager** ensures that the proof is planned, measured against defined exit criteria, assembled into an evidence pack, and translated into a bounded release decision that governance can defend.

That is the difference between technical testing and accountable AI delivery.

Exhibit 8D — What Must Be Proven Before Scale

Before an AI system scales, the organization should be able to prove:

Performance
The system performs acceptably on representative work.

Limits
Known failure modes and boundary conditions are documented.

Safety and trustworthiness
The system is valid, reliable, and appropriately safe for the use case.

Security
Material abuse paths and exploit conditions have been tested and mitigated.

Human oversight
Humans can understand, review, override, and escalate where required.

Operational readiness
The workflow, monitoring, rollback, and support model are ready.

Residual risk
Unresolved risks are visible, accepted at the right level, and not hidden inside optimism.

If these cannot be shown, the system may still be interesting. It has not yet earned the right to scale.

Red Flags

Validation is probably weak when:

- test results are mostly benchmark or demo based
- scenarios are not representative of real use
- governance sees results only at the end
- technical testing is strong but business validation is weak
- exit criteria were defined after the pilot
- security testing is treated as separate from functional validation
- override behavior is not analyzed
- field testing is skipped because the demo looked good
- known limitations are buried
- the project cannot produce a single coherent evidence pack

These are signs that the organization is testing activity, not release readiness.

Checklist Callout — Before You Approve Scale

Before approving broader deployment, ask:

What has been tested?
What has been validated in real conditions?
What important conditions were not tested?
What evidence shows the system is fit for purpose?
What do override and user-friction signals tell us?
What critical security or integrity risks remain?
Who reviewed the evidence?
Who accepts the residual risk?
What post-launch metrics will prove that scale is still deserved?

If those questions do not have clear answers, the system is not ready for scale.

Key Takeaway

AI does not earn the right to scale through demos, optimism, or isolated benchmark wins.

It earns that right through disciplined validation, representative testing, structured evidence, and clear governance decisions based on what the evidence does and does not show.

Technical teams are essential because they generate much of the proof.
The AI Project Manager is essential because the proof must be organized, traced, challenged, staged, and turned into a release decision the enterprise can defend.

That is what separates technical activity from accountable AI delivery.

References

1. NIST, *Artificial Intelligence Risk Management Framework (AI RMF 1.0)* — source for lifecycle TEVV, trustworthiness characteristics, objective and documented TEVV processes, and the role of multiple AI actors across the lifecycle.

2. NIST, *Artificial Intelligence Risk Management Framework: Generative Artificial Intelligence Profile* — source for GAI-specific lifecycle risk management, pre-deployment testing limits, structured public feedback, field testing, red-teaming, override monitoring, staged release, and real-world evaluation.

3. OWASP, *Top 10 for Large Language Model Applications* — source for prompt injection, insecure output handling, training data poisoning, model denial of service, supply-chain vulnerabilities, sensitive information disclosure, and insecure plugin design as validation-relevant risk categories.

4. ISO, *ISO/IEC 42001:2023 — AI management systems* — source for AI management as a structured, continually improving system of policies, objectives, processes, and monitoring.

Chapter 9 — Operating Model, Roles, and RACI: Who Actually Makes AI Delivery Work

AI projects do not fail only because models underperform.

They also fail because nobody is quite sure who owns what.

The sponsor assumes the delivery team will handle it.
The data team assumes the business owns the definitions.
The security team assumes someone else approved the use of sensitive content.
The operations team inherits a system it did not help design.
The technical team proves the model can work, but no one has organized the decisions, dependencies, approvals, and handoffs required to make the system work in the enterprise.

That is not a technical failure.

It is an operating-model failure.

Once the business case, readiness, governance, and validation work are in place, the next question is practical:

Who actually makes AI delivery work day to day?

This chapter answers that question.

Why the Operating Model Matters

The major frameworks all point in the same direction: AI requires defined roles, responsibilities, and lifecycle management, not just technical talent. NIST's AI RMF says governance should establish policies that define AI risk-management roles and responsibilities for positions directly and indirectly related to AI systems, explicitly including senior management, product management, project management, AI development, human-AI interaction, and AI testing and evaluation. ISO/IEC 42001 similarly frames AI management as an organizational system with policies, objectives, processes, responsibilities, and continual improvement. The EU AI Act is also role-based, placing different obligations on providers and deployers rather than treating "the organization" as a single undifferentiated actor.

The practical implication is simple:

An AI project needs an operating model before it needs heroics.

Without one, accountability fragments, handoffs fail, and the project becomes dependent on informal relationships and individual effort.

The AI Operating Model Is Not the Same as the Software Operating Model

Many organizations assume they can reuse their normal software delivery model with minor adjustments.

Sometimes that is enough for a low-risk assistive feature. Often it is not.

AI delivery usually adds:

- data owners and knowledge owners
- model or prompt owners
- evaluation and validation roles
- human-oversight design
- monitoring for drift, groundedness, and misuse
- stronger security and risk review
- more frequent change review
- post-launch performance interpretation that is less binary than traditional software testing

That means the delivery model cannot rely on the old assumption that requirements are fixed, outputs are deterministic, and testing is mainly about confirming that code behaves exactly as specified.

AI introduces probability, ambiguity, evolving sources, and model behavior that must be managed rather than merely implemented.

So, the operating model has to do two things at once:

- deliver a working system
- continuously coordinate risk, evidence, and ownership across the lifecycle

That is where the **AI Project Manager** becomes critical.

The Role of the AI Project Manager

The AI Project Manager is not just a generic project manager with a new label.

In an AI initiative, this role has to manage a delivery environment where:

- requirements evolve through experimentation
- data readiness and process readiness affect scope
- validation evidence matters as much as build progress
- governance gates shape release decisions
- technical and nontechnical stakeholders interpret success differently
- model, retrieval, prompt, and workflow changes can all alter risk

PMI's current AI materials make the profession's direction explicit: project professionals are expected to both use AI in project work and lead AI-driven transformations, and PMI emphasizes skills such as data literacy, trustworthy AI practices, and agile delivery for AI contexts. NIST's AI RMF Playbook also explicitly includes **project management** among the roles for which AI risk-management responsibilities should be defined.

That means the AI Project Manager is not replacing technical leadership. The role is different.

The AI Project Manager is the person who:

- keeps the use case tied to business outcomes
- ensures dependencies across data, model, workflow, security, and operations are visible
- turns governance requirements into delivery tasks and gates
- makes validation evidence decision-ready
- manages scope, residual risk, and stakeholder alignment
- ensures the project does not drift into a technically interesting but operationally unusable outcome

The model team may optimize performance.
The security team may test resilience.
The product owner may shape features.
The data team may improve pipelines.
The AI Project Manager makes sure these streams come together into a governed, deliverable whole.

The AI Project Manager Is Distinct from AI Technical Resources

This distinction should be explicit in the book.

AI technical resources are primarily responsible for designing, building, evaluating, and improving the technical solution:

- data scientists
- ML engineers
- software engineers
- prompt engineers
- platform engineers
- data engineers
- evaluators
- security testers

The AI Project Manager is primarily responsible for managing the **delivery system** around that work:

- integrated plan
- stage-gate readiness
- risk and issue coordination
- dependency management
- evidence tracking
- stakeholder alignment
- decision support for sponsors and governance bodies
- transition into operations

Technical resources answer:
"What did we build?"
"How does it perform?"
"What changed in the model or pipeline?"

The AI Project Manager helps the organization answer:
"Are we ready for the next gate?"
"What is blocking safe scale?"
"Who owns this unresolved issue?"
"What evidence supports the decision?"
"What remains risky, and who accepts it?"

That is not a minor distinction. It is one of the defining characteristics of professional AI delivery.

Exhibit 9A — What the AI Project Manager Owns That Technical Teams Usually Do Not

The AI Project Manager should typically own or orchestrate:

Delivery integration
Combining business, data, model, governance, security, and operations work into one delivery path.

Decision readiness
Making sure sponsors and review bodies receive clear options, evidence, assumptions, open risks, and gate recommendations.

Dependency management
Tracking what the use case depends on across systems, teams, policies, vendors, and workflow changes.

Risk and issue management
Not just technical defects, but unresolved ownership, weak readiness, incomplete controls, unvalidated assumptions, and operational handoff gaps.

Evidence orchestration
Ensuring that testing, validation, pilot findings, and monitoring design are translated into a release-quality evidence pack.

Cross-functional accountability
Making sure tasks do not disappear into organizational seams.

This is why the AI Project Manager is not a project scheduler with a more fashionable title. The role is a control point in the delivery system.

The Minimum Roles in an AI Delivery Operating Model

Not every organization needs the same org chart. But most enterprise AI initiatives need the same minimum role types, even if one person covers more than one role in smaller settings.

These roles are usually required:

Executive sponsor
Owns strategic sponsorship, funding support, and top-level escalation.

Business owner
Owns the use case, business outcomes, adoption expectations, and value realization.

AI Project Manager
Owns integrated delivery coordination, gate readiness, dependency management, and decision support.

Product or capability owner
Owns feature priorities, user experience trade-offs, backlog shaping, and value sequencing.

Technical lead or solution lead
Owns the technical solution path, architecture trade-offs, and engineering delivery.

Data owner
Owns source authority, semantics, access, and data-use constraints.

Model / prompt / retrieval owner
Owns technical behavior of the AI layer, depending on the architecture.

Security and privacy leads
Own controls, security review, data protection expectations, and incident escalation paths.

Validation / evaluation lead
Owns the test strategy, measurement logic, and evidence quality.

Operational owner
Owns production monitoring, support, rollback readiness, and service continuity after launch.

Human oversight owner
Owns real-world review responsibilities where human intervention remains required.

Governance / review authority
Owns higher-risk approval, exceptions, and policy interpretation when the project crosses control boundaries.

NIST's governance guidance supports exactly this kind of role definition by calling for responsibilities across management, product, project, design, development, human-AI interaction, and testing functions.

The Best Operating Model Is Usually Federated, Not Centralized

Organizations often swing between two extremes.

One extreme is full centralization: one AI team tries to own everything.
The other is full decentralization: each business function improvises its own AI delivery pattern.

Both models create problems.

A better pattern is usually **federated**:

- central governance and shared standards
- local business ownership of use cases
- shared platform, security, and review capabilities
- distributed delivery teams close to the workflow

This matches the logic of both NIST and ISO/IEC 42001, which emphasize organization-wide governance with defined responsibilities rather than either total centralization or total fragmentation.

In practical terms, a federated model often means:

- enterprise rules are set centrally
- use cases are owned in the business
- shared services support model/platform/security capabilities
- the AI Project Manager coordinates across the federation

That helps the organization avoid two common failures:

- bottlenecking all AI through a small central team
- letting every team reinvent governance, testing, and control practices separately

RACI Is Especially Important in AI Projects

Traditional projects can survive some role ambiguity.

AI projects survive it less well.

That is because AI creates more overlap zones:

- who owns model behavior versus business outcomes
- who owns source quality versus retrieval quality
- who owns validation criteria versus technical evaluation
- who owns pilot exit decisions versus production support readiness
- who owns incidents when a failure spans model, data, workflow, and user behavior

That is why a clear RACI is not optional decoration. It is part of the operating model.

A useful AI RACI should cover at least:

- use-case approval
- business-case approval
- data readiness
- process readiness
- model / prompt / retrieval design
- security and privacy review
- validation planning
- pilot exit approval
- production release approval
- production monitoring
- incident response
- major change review
- retirement / decommissioning

Exhibit 9B — Sample RACI for an Enterprise AI Use Case

Role key:
ES Executive Sponsor | BO Business Owner | PM AI Project Manager | PO Product Owner | AI TL Technical Lead (AI Solution Lead) | DL Data Lead / Data Owner | VL Validation Lead | SP Security / Privacy | OO Operations Owner | GA Governance Authority

R = Responsible | A = Accountable | C = Consulted | I = Informed

9B-1. Delivery and release

Activity	ES	BO	PM	PO	AI TL	DL	VL	SP	OO	GA
Use-case selection	A	R	C	C	C	C	I	I	I	C
Business case	I	A/R	R	C	C	C	I	I	C	I
Data/process readiness	I	A	R	C	C	R	C	C	C	I
AI solution design	I	C	C	A/R	R	C	C	C	I	I
Source approval	I	C	C	I	C	A/R	I	C	I	I
Security/privacy review	I	C	C	I	C	C	I	A/R	I	C
Validation plan / exit criteria	I	C	A/R	C	C	C	R	C	C	I
Pilot execution	I	C	A/R	C	R	C	R	C	C	I
Pilot exit recommendation	I	C	A/R	C	C	C	R	C	C	C
Production release*	I	A	R	C	C	C	C	C	C	A/R*

9B-2. Run, change, and retirement

Activity	ES	BO	PM	PO	AI TL	DL	VL	SP	OO	GA
Post-launch monitoring	I	A	C	I	C	C	C	C	R	I
Incident response	I	A	C	I	R	C	C	R	R	I
Major change review*	I	C	A/R	C	R	C	C	C	C	C/A*
Revalidation / reapproval	I	C	A/R	I	C	C	R	C	C	A
Retirement / decommissioning	I	A	R	I	C	C	C	C	R	C

Note:
*** Depending on risk tier, accountability for Production Release and Major Change Review may sit with the Business Owner, Governance Authority, or both.**

Short role definitions for the chapter

AI TL (Technical Lead / AI Solution Lead): Owns AI solution design and technical delivery, including model, prompt, retrieval, orchestration, integration, and engineering trade-offs.

DL (Data Lead / Data Owner): Owns source authority, semantics, access, freshness, lineage, and approved use of enterprise data or knowledge sources.

That means the AI Project Manager often becomes the role most responsible for preventing the project from failing in silence.

When ownership is fuzzy, the AI Project Manager should surface it.
When evidence is incomplete, the AI Project Manager should make that visible before the gate.
When business expectations outrun technical readiness, the AI Project Manager should force the conversation.
When technical teams optimize the wrong thing, the AI Project Manager should reconnect the work to the use case and the gate criteria.
When operations is not ready to inherit the system, the AI Project Manager should stop the illusion that "delivery is complete."

This is one reason PMI's framing is useful: project professionals are not just end users of AI tools. They are leading AI-enabled transformation and the project management of AI transformations.

Handoffs Matter More in AI Projects

Many project failures happen at handoff points.

In AI, the most dangerous handoffs are often:

- business to data
- design to validation
- pilot to production
- delivery to operations
- governance approval to runtime monitoring

A mature operating model should make those handoffs explicit.

For each handoff, the team should know:

- what artifacts must be complete
- what evidence must exist
- what risks remain open
- who accepts them
- what support model takes over
- what triggers escalation after transition

The AI Project Manager should normally own the orchestration of these handoffs, even when the receiving function owns the ongoing work afterward.

The Operating Model Must Extend Beyond Launch

An AI operating model that ends at go-live is incomplete.

ISO/IEC 42001's emphasis on maintaining and continually improving an AI management system reinforces this point. The EU AI Act's distinction between providers and deployers also reflects a lifecycle view: obligations do not end at release, because operation, monitoring, transparency, and oversight continue after deployment.

That means the operating model should define not just build roles, but run roles:

- who reviews monitoring results
- who investigates drift

- who approves major prompt or model changes
- who owns reindexing or retraining decisions
- who handles incidents
- who approves rollback or retirement

If these are left vague, launch becomes a handoff into confusion.

Exhibit 9C — Operating Model Questions the AI Project Manager Should Force Early

Before delivery gets too far, the AI Project Manager should push the team to answer:

Who owns the business outcome?
Who owns the data and knowledge sources?
Who owns the model, prompt, or retrieval behavior?
Who defines validation criteria?
Who signs off on pilot exit?
Who owns production monitoring?
Who is on point when an incident spans model, workflow, and source content?
Who approves material changes after launch?
Who decides when the system should be paused or retired?

If the answer to several of these is "we'll figure it out later," the operating model is not ready.

Common Role Failures

AI delivery usually weakens when one of these patterns appears:

The technical team becomes the de facto business owner.
This often happens when the business delegates too much and later complains that the output is "not what we needed."

The business owner is named but not active.
Accountability without participation is decorative.

Governance is centralized, but delivery is not integrated.
The project keeps moving, but approvals arrive late and feel disconnected from the work.

Operations is engaged too late.
The system reaches release with no realistic owner for runtime monitoring and support.

The AI Project Manager is treated as an administrator instead of a delivery integrator.
This strips the role of the authority needed to coordinate evidence, dependencies, and decisions.

Human oversight is assigned vaguely.
Everyone assumes someone will catch issues, but no one is explicitly responsible.

These are not personality problems. They are operating-model defects.

Completed Example — Operating Model for AI-Assisted Ticket Triage

Consider the recurring ticket-triage example.

A weak operating model would assign the work mainly to the technical automation team, ask the service desk to review it near the end, and involve security and operations only when production release is close. The result would likely be the same familiar pattern: progress looks good, but ownership questions surface late, validation criteria are incomplete, and operational handoff becomes stressful.

A stronger operating model would look like this:

Executive sponsor
VP, Enterprise Support Services

Business owner
Director, Service Operations

AI Project Manager
Owns integrated delivery plan, risk and issue coordination, gate readiness, evidence pack assembly, and cross-functional dependency management

Product owner
Support automation product lead

Technical lead
Lead architect for service automation and AI routing

Data owner
Service management platform owner

Validation lead
QA / evaluation lead for routing quality and pilot measurement

Security lead
Application and data security reviewer

Operational owner
Service desk operations manager

Human oversight owner
Service desk lead group responsible for override and escalation during pilot and controlled production

Under this model, the AI Project Manager is not writing the routing logic or calibrating the classifier. But the AI Project Manager does ensure that:

- the business owner signs off on scope and expected value
- the data owner confirms authoritative routing rules and taxonomy changes
- the validation lead defines pilot exit criteria before testing starts
- the security lead's review is scheduled in time to matter
- the operational owner accepts monitoring, override, and rollback procedures before release
- the governance body receives a complete, coherent release recommendation rather than scattered findings

That is what a functioning operating model looks like.

The system succeeds not because everyone works harder, but because everyone knows their role before the pressure arrives.

Red Flags

The operating model is probably weak when:

- the project cannot name a true business owner
- the AI Project Manager is reduced to status reporting only
- technical teams are left to interpret business risk on their own
- validation ownership is unclear
- operations joins only near release
- governance is treated as external to delivery
- multiple teams believe someone else owns the same decision

- major handoffs have no artifacts or entry criteria
- incident responsibility after launch is vague
- no one owns change approval after go-live

When several of these are present, the problem is not execution discipline alone. The structure itself is wrong.

Checklist Callout — Before You Finalize the AI Operating Model

Before the project moves too far, ask:

Who owns the business outcome?
Who owns delivery integration?
Who owns data and source authority?
Who owns technical behavior?
Who owns validation?
Who owns production operations?
Who owns human oversight?
Who owns incident response?
Who owns major change approval?
Does the AI Project Manager have enough authority to coordinate across all of them?

If these questions do not have clear answers, the project may still move. It will not move cleanly.

Key Takeaway

AI delivery works when the operating model makes accountability visible.

That means clear roles, explicit handoffs, real ownership, and a RACI that covers not just build activities, but validation, monitoring, incident response, change control, and retirement.

The AI Project Manager is central to that model, not because the role replaces technical expertise, but because AI delivery fails when technical work, business decisions, governance expectations, and operational reality are not integrated into one managed system.

That is what the AI Project Manager is there to do.

References

1. NIST, *Artificial Intelligence Risk Management Framework (AI RMF 1.0)* — source for lifecycle governance and AI actors across management, product, project, design, development, human-AI interaction, and testing.

2. NIST AI RMF Playbook, *Govern* — source explicitly calling for policies that define AI risk-management roles and responsibilities, including project management.

3. ISO, *ISO 42001 explained* and *ISO/IEC 42001:2023 — AI management systems* — source for AI management systems with defined responsibilities, processes, and continual improvement.

4. European Commission, *AI Act | Shaping Europe's digital future* and *Navigating the AI Act* — source for the Act's risk-based structure, provider/deployer responsibilities, staged applicability, and ongoing lifecycle obligations.

5. PMI, *Artificial Intelligence in Project Management* and *Skills Every Project Manager Needs to Lead in Artificial Intelligence* — source for the evolving role of project professionals in leading AI transformation and the project management of AI initiatives.

Chapter 10

Change Management, Adoption, and Human Trust: Why a Technically Sound AI System Still Fails Without Behavioral Uptake

An AI system can be technically sound and still fail.

It can be accurate enough, fast enough, secure enough, and even governance-approved — and still fail because people do not use it, do not trust it, over trust it, work around it, or never change their behavior in the way the business case assumed.

That is why change management in AI cannot be treated as a generic communications plan.

AI changes work differently from ordinary software.

Traditional systems usually ask people to follow a defined process more consistently. AI systems ask people to do something harder: to work with a probabilistic system, interpret uncertain outputs, exercise judgment about when to trust or challenge it, and adapt their workflow as the system learns, changes, or is refined over time. NIST's Generative AI Profile treats this as a distinct human-AI configuration risk and explicitly warns about algorithmic aversion, automation bias or over-reliance, misalignment of goals, and other failure modes that arise from how humans and AI systems interact rather than from model quality alone.

That is why this chapter must stay focused on **AI-specific** change management, not generic transformation language.

The question is not simply, "How do we communicate the change?"

The question is: **How do we create the right human behaviors around a system that is useful, fallible, evolving, and influential?**

The Core Argument

In AI delivery, adoption is not a soft issue that sits outside the technical program.

It is part of the control environment.

A system that people underuse may never realize value.
A system that people over trust may create hidden risk.
A system that people use inconsistently may distort the business case and the monitoring

evidence.
A system that changes workflow without redesigning roles may create friction, shadow work, or silent noncompliance.

This is one reason the major frameworks increasingly connect trust, oversight, literacy, monitoring, and human roles. NIST ties trustworthy AI to governance, risk management, and the human-AI configuration. The EU AI Act's current guidance says deployers of high-risk AI systems must monitor operation, act on identified risks or serious incidents, and assign human oversight to a person in the organization who is sufficiently equipped and enabled to exercise it. OECD's workplace guidance similarly warns that even where human oversight exists, there is a risk of mere "rubber-stamping" of AI decisions.

That means human uptake is not just an HR matter.

It is a delivery matter, a governance matter, and often a safety matter.

Why AI Change Management Is Different

Generic change management assumes a more stable kind of change. A new platform, a new workflow, a new reporting tool, or a new policy can usually be explained in terms of standardization, compliance, and future-state process adoption.

AI introduces additional dynamics that make behavior harder to manage.

First, AI systems are often **probabilistic rather than deterministic**. People must learn that a useful system can still be wrong sometimes.

Second, AI systems often appear more capable than they are. Fluent answers, natural language interaction, and polished summaries can create confidence beyond what the evidence supports. NIST explicitly identifies this as part of human-AI configuration risk, including automation bias and over-reliance.

Third, AI systems often require **trust calibration**, not just trust-building. The goal is not maximum trust. The goal is appropriate trust.

Fourth, AI changes work at the level of **judgment and decision behavior**, not just task sequence. It changes how people review, escalate, approve, challenge, summarize, and prioritize.

Fifth, AI systems keep evolving. Models change, prompts change, retrieval sources change, and thresholds change. That means adoption is not a one-time transition. It is a managed relationship between people and a changing system.

This is why AI programs often struggle even when the technology works. They have treated behavioral uptake as if it were generic software adoption when it is actually an exercise in human judgment design.

Exhibit 10A — What Makes AI Adoption Different from Generic Change

AI change management must address five dynamics that generic change methods often underplay.

1. Trust calibration
Users must learn when to trust, when to verify, and when to escalate.

2. Human-AI interaction risk
Over-reliance, under-reliance, rubber-stamping, and disengagement are all real failure modes.

3. Role redesign
AI changes who reviews, who decides, who checks, and what work remains distinctly human.

4. AI literacy
Users need enough understanding to interpret outputs, limits, confidence, and failure modes.

5. Continuous adaptation
Because AI systems evolve, adoption and behavior must be revalidated over time, not assumed after launch.

If these are ignored, technically strong systems often stall or create new risk.

Trust Is Not the Same as Usage

One of the easiest mistakes in AI programs is to confuse usage with trust.

A team may log in frequently because leadership told them to.
A reviewer may approve AI recommendations because it is faster.
An employee may copy AI-generated text into a workflow while privately distrusting it.
Another employee may abandon the system after two visible mistakes, even if the measured accuracy is acceptable overall.

None of those behaviors can be understood from usage metrics alone.

The organization needs to know:

- when users rely on the system
- when they ignore it
- when they override it
- when they verify it
- when they rubber-stamp it
- when they create shadow work to compensate for it
- when they quietly route around it

OECD's workplace guidance is especially useful here because it warns that "human in the loop" arrangements can still fail through rubber-stamping, and it emphasizes meaningful human input, oversight, and accountability in decisions that affect people. It also notes evidence that workplace outcomes are more positive in firms that consult workers about the adoption of new technologies.

That means AI adoption metrics should not stop at logins or task counts. They should include **behavioral quality**.

The Two Failure Modes: Over trust and Under trust

AI adoption usually fails in one of two directions.

The first is **under trust**. People dismiss the system too quickly, continue to work manually, and never let the AI contribute enough to create measurable value. This often happens when the system is introduced with too little evidence, too little user context, or too much hype.

The second is **over trust**. People stop checking outputs they should still be checking. Oversight becomes symbolic. Review becomes perfunctory. AI recommendations begin to substitute for judgment instead of informing it.

NIST's GAI Profile explicitly names these risks in its discussion of human-AI configuration, including algorithmic aversion and automation bias or over-reliance.

A mature AI change strategy should try to prevent both.

That is why the objective is not "make people trust the AI."
The objective is "help people trust it appropriately."

AI Literacy Is a Change Requirement, Not an Optional Training Topic

Because AI changes work through judgment, oversight, and interpretation, literacy matters more than in many traditional rollouts.

Users need to understand:

- what the system is supposed to do
- what it is not supposed to do
- what evidence supports its outputs
- what its failure modes look like
- what escalation path exists
- what must still be checked by a human
- what the consequences are of getting it wrong

This is not optional background knowledge. The EU AI Act's literacy obligations became applicable on February 2, 2025, and the European Commission states that providers and deployers should ensure a sufficient level of AI literacy among staff and others dealing with AI on their behalf, taking account of context and the persons affected.

For enterprise delivery, the practical lesson is broader than regulation:

Without AI literacy, change management becomes guesswork.

People cannot adopt responsibly what they do not understand well enough to challenge.

That means role-based literacy is essential. A frontline reviewer needs something different from an executive sponsor. A service desk lead needs something different from a data owner. A human oversight owner needs something different from a casual business user.

Workflow Redesign Matters More Than Awareness Campaigns

Many AI rollouts focus too much on messaging and not enough on workflow redesign.

That is especially dangerous in AI.

If the new system changes who is expected to verify, when exceptions are escalated, how confidence is interpreted, what artifacts are retained, or what tasks are now machine-supported, then the workflow has changed whether the organization admits it or not.

A weak adoption program says:
"Please use the new AI assistant."

A stronger adoption program says:
"When the system produces a cited answer, here is when you can rely on it, when you must verify it, when you must escalate it, and how your role has changed."

AI-specific change management should therefore answer:

- What human step is being removed?
- What human step is being added?
- What human step is being narrowed?
- What evidence must a person review before acting?
- What override behavior is expected?
- What should users do when the system is uncertain or conflicting?
- What should users do when the system appears confident but is wrong?

This is how change management becomes operational rather than rhetorical.

Exhibit 10B — What the Adoption Design Must Specify

Before launch, the AI program should specify:

Who uses the system
Which role groups are in scope, and for what tasks?

How they should use it
What is assistive, what is reviewable, and what remains human-only?

When they must verify
What conditions require checking, escalation, or abstention?

What counts as correct behavior
What does appropriate reliance actually look like?

What evidence they see
Citations, explanations, confidence indicators, logs, or decision support artifacts.

What happens when they disagree with the system
Override, appeal, escalation, feedback, or temporary fallback.

If these are vague, adoption becomes inconsistent and unsafe.

Consultation Matters More in AI Than in Many Other Changes

This is another place where generic change language can mislead.

In many standard transformations, user consultation is beneficial. In AI, it is often essential because the technology changes judgment, autonomy, and perceived fairness in ways that directly affect how people experience work.

OECD's workplace guidance states that outcomes are more positive in firms that consult workers about the adoption of new technologies, and its more recent compendium on human-centered AI adoption emphasizes consultation, upskilling, workplace guidelines, and social dialogue as part of safe and trustworthy AI adoption at work.

That does not mean every AI use case requires formal labor consultation in every jurisdiction. It does mean the project should not assume that user acceptance will follow automatically from technical quality.

People want to know:

- whether AI changes their judgment or autonomy
- whether it is evaluating them
- whether they are accountable for its mistakes
- whether the oversight role is real or symbolic
- whether their feedback will be used
- whether the system was designed with actual work conditions in mind

In AI, consultation is not merely a courtesy. It is often part of making the system usable and trusted.

Human Oversight Must Be Real in Practice

A common failure pattern in AI rollout is to declare human oversight in policy but not make it workable in practice.

The reviewer may not have enough time.
The interface may not provide enough evidence.
The confidence signals may be weak or misleading.
The escalation path may be too slow.
The person may not know what they are responsible for.
The override process may be too cumbersome to use well.

The EU AI Act guidance says deployers of high-risk AI systems must assign human oversight to a person in the organization and that this person must be sufficiently equipped and enabled to exercise it. OECD separately warns that human-in-the-loop arrangements can still degrade into rubber-stamping.

That means AI adoption should measure not just whether oversight exists on paper, but whether it works in practice.

If the human reviewer cannot intervene meaningfully, then change management has not solved the problem. It has only renamed it.

Feedback and Recourse Are Part of Adoption

AI change management is weaker when users have no clear way to challenge outputs, report issues, or ask for recourse.

NIST's GAI Profile recommends establishing mechanisms or channels for users, experts, or community members to provide feedback, adjudicating and implementing relevant feedback at a regular cadence, and providing thorough instructions so users understand feedback and recourse mechanisms.

That matters because AI systems fail in patterns users often notice before dashboards do:

- odd but plausible answers
- repeated drift in one domain
- escalating caution among experienced reviewers
- unexpected user workarounds

- inconsistent behavior under similar prompts or cases
- confidence without evidence

A mature AI adoption design therefore includes:

- a visible feedback path
- clear expectations for what should be reported
- response ownership
- a regular review cadence
- evidence that the organization actually acts on what it hears

If user feedback disappears into a void, trust declines fast.

The AI Project Manager's Role in Adoption

This chapter is also one more place where the AI Project Manager should be visible as distinct from technical resources.

The technical team can explain the model, fix issues, improve prompts, and refine retrieval behavior.

But the AI Project Manager is the person who should ensure that:

- adoption assumptions in the business case are visible
- the right user groups are prepared before launch
- workflow redesign is explicit
- oversight roles are defined and staffed
- literacy is role-based
- feedback loops are operational
- adoption metrics include behavior, not just access
- sponsors understand the difference between usage and trust
- post-launch evidence includes overrides, friction, and recourse trends

This is not a generic enablement function. It is delivery integration applied to human uptake.

The AI Project Manager helps prevent one of the most common enterprise mistakes: treating adoption as a post-technical activity rather than as part of the design of the AI system itself.

Exhibit 10C — The AI Project Manager's Adoption Responsibilities

In an AI program, the AI Project Manager should typically orchestrate:

Adoption assumptions
Linking business-case value assumptions to actual user behaviors that must change.

Readiness of role groups
Ensuring that reviewers, operators, approvers, and end users know what changes for them.

Behavioral gate criteria
Defining what must be true for pilot exit or broader rollout, including override patterns and trust signals.

Feedback loops
Making sure adoption issues, user complaints, and recourse signals have owners and review cadence.

Cross-functional handoffs
Connecting technical teams, business owners, oversight owners, and operations so the user experience is governed, not improvised.

Post-launch adoption evidence
Tracking not just usage, but calibration, workarounds, friction, and reliance patterns.

This is part of AI delivery, not an extra.

What to Measure After Launch

Once AI goes live, the organization needs to look beyond standard rollout metrics.

Useful AI-specific adoption measures often include:

- override rate
- verification rate
- abstention frequency

- escalation frequency
- user reliance by task type
- citation use or evidence-check behavior where relevant
- repeat-use by experienced users, not just first-time trials
- shadow-work indicators
- user-reported confidence and distrust patterns
- time saved only where verified by real workflow behavior
- differential uptake across teams or roles
- near misses caused by over-reliance or under-reliance

These are the measures that reveal whether adoption is becoming healthy or hazardous.

A system with rising usage but rising rubber-stamping may be getting more dangerous.
A system with moderate usage but strong calibration and stable oversight may be becoming more trustworthy.

That is why AI adoption metrics must stay tied to governance and evidence, not drift into vanity metrics.

Completed Example — Adoption and Trust in AI-Assisted Ticket Triage

Consider again the AI-assisted ticket-triage use case.

A generic rollout might train the service desk on the interface, announce the productivity benefits, and track how many people use the tool.

An AI-specific rollout would do more.

It would first identify the changed behaviors that matter:

- when analysts should rely on the suggested route
- when they must review it carefully
- when a high-priority ticket must always trigger human confirmation
- how overrides should be coded

- how unusual or misleading summaries should be reported
- how confidence thresholds should be interpreted
- what users must do when team ownership changes are not reflected in the system

The rollout would include role-based literacy for service desk analysts, service desk leads, and operations managers. It would provide concrete examples of safe reliance, unsafe reliance, and when escalation is required. It would define the feedback path and explain how override data will be reviewed.

The pilot would then measure not only routing improvement, but also behavioral evidence:

- override rate by week
- override reasons
- high-priority verification behavior
- analyst confidence patterns
- time saved only where the workflow actually moved faster
- whether users bypassed the AI in certain ticket categories
- whether leads felt oversight was real or symbolic

A mature rollout might show this pattern:

- usage reaches **92 percent** among in-scope analysts by the end of week 6
- override rate declines from **29 percent** in week 1 to **18 percent** by week 6
- high-priority tickets still receive human verification in **98 percent** of required cases
- analysts report highest trust in routine incidents and lowest trust in ambiguous cross-team routing
- operations review finds that a subset of analysts are bypassing the AI for incomplete tickets, which leads to a refinement of prompt handling and user guidance
- time saved is real in routine categories, but not yet realized in more ambiguous categories

That is a much better adoption story than "people are using the tool."

It shows calibrated trust, targeted redesign, active feedback, and evidence-based learning.

And in that story, the AI Project Manager is not the person who tuned the classifier. The AI Project Manager is the person who ensured the rollout measured the right behavioral conditions and converted them into a decision about whether broader deployment was justified.

Red Flags

AI change management is probably weak when:

- the rollout plan sounds like a standard software launch
- training focuses on features but not judgment
- trust is discussed only as "buy-in"
- oversight is assumed rather than practiced
- usage is measured but override behavior is ignored
- consultation happens too late
- users have no clear recourse path
- the project never defines what appropriate reliance looks like
- leadership expects adoption without workflow redesign
- the AI Project Manager is not involved in adoption evidence

These are signs that the organization is treating AI as a tool rollout rather than a change in human-machine work.

Checklist Callout — Before You Call Adoption "Done"

Before declaring the rollout successful, ask:

Do users know when to trust the AI and when to verify it?
Is human oversight real in practice?
Do role groups understand how their work has changed?
Do users have a visible feedback and recourse path?
Are override and friction signals being reviewed?
Are workers or frontline users being consulted in a meaningful way?

Is the organization measuring calibration, not just usage?
Have adoption assumptions in the business case actually become visible behaviors?
Is the AI Project Manager tracking these signals as part of delivery, not as an afterthought?

If the answer to several of these is no, the system may be live. Adoption is not complete.

Key Takeaway

AI change management is not generic change management with new branding.

It is the discipline of shaping the right human behaviors around a useful but fallible system. That means calibrating trust, redesigning workflows, building AI literacy, making oversight real, creating feedback and recourse, and measuring adoption in terms of behavior rather than mere access.

A technically sound AI system still fails when behavioral uptake is weak or mis-calibrated.

That is why human trust is not a soft topic at the edge of the project.

It is one of the conditions under which AI earns the right to remain in use.

References

1. NIST, *Artificial Intelligence Risk Management Framework: Generative Artificial Intelligence Profile* — source for human-AI configuration risk, including algorithmic aversion, automation bias or over-reliance, the need for policies on human-AI oversight, critical-thinking and safety-first culture, and feedback and recourse mechanisms.

2. NIST, *Artificial Intelligence Risk Management Framework (AI RMF 1.0)* — source for trustworthiness and lifecycle risk management for AI systems.

3. European Commission, *AI Act | Shaping Europe's digital future* — source for AI literacy applicability and lifecycle obligations under the AI Act.

4. European Commission, *Navigating the AI Act* — source for current guidance that deployers must monitor operation, act on risks or serious incidents, and assign human oversight to sufficiently equipped and enabled persons; also, source for workplace information duties in certain cases.

5. OECD, *Using AI in the Workplace* — source for meaningful human input, rubber-stamping risk in human-in-the-loop systems, and the value of accountability in workplace AI use.

6. OECD, *Compendium of Best Practices for the Human-Centered Adoption of Safe, Secure and Trustworthy AI in the World of Work* — source for human-centered AI adoption, upskilling, workplace guidelines, and consultation/social dialogue in AI adoption.

Part 3-Running the AI Project

Chapter 11

Planning for Uncertainty and Experimentation

Why AI planning is different

Traditional projects are often planned around a relatively stable assumption: the team knows what it is trying to build, how success will be judged, and what sequence of work is required to get there. AI projects rarely offer that level of certainty.

In AI delivery, the organization may not yet know whether the use case is technically viable at the required quality level, whether the available data is fit for purpose, whether the workflow can absorb the AI effectively, or whether users will trust the output enough to use it. That does not mean planning is impossible. It means planning must be built differently.

The AI Project Manager's job is not to pretend uncertainty does not exist. It is to structure uncertainty so the project can still move with discipline.

That is the core idea of this chapter: AI projects should not be planned as if all answers are already known, but neither should they be run as open-ended experimentation. The AI Project Manager must create a delivery structure that allows learning, testing, and adjustment without losing accountability, timeline control, or decision clarity.

The AI Project Manager's role in uncertain work

In an AI project, uncertainty is not just a risk to be listed in a log. It is a defining feature of the delivery environment.

That means the AI Project Manager must do more than create schedules and coordinate meetings. The role must help the organization answer a different set of planning questions:

What assumptions are still unproven?

What must be learned before the project can progress responsibly?

What decisions will depend on the answers?

What evidence will be accepted as good enough?

What happens if the evidence is weak or mixed?

These questions matter because uncertainty becomes dangerous when it stays vague. When uncertainty is unstructured, teams continue working without knowing what they are actually proving, executives assume progress means feasibility, and projects drift forward on effort rather than evidence.

The AI Project Manager helps prevent that by converting uncertainty into a sequence of learning objectives, experiments, review points, and decision gates.

Planning must separate known work from unknown work

One of the most helpful disciplines in AI planning is separating work that is relatively predictable from work that is genuinely exploratory.

Some tasks in an AI project are still quite plannable. Stakeholder alignment, governance reviews, security engagement, vendor coordination, workflow mapping, change planning, training development, and reporting cadence can usually be planned with reasonable confidence.

Other tasks are less certain. Model performance may be unclear. Data usefulness may be uncertain. Prompt behavior may vary. Human-review thresholds may need testing. Retrieval quality may be inconsistent. Business fit may depend on real usage patterns that cannot be fully predicted in advance.

The AI Project Manager should not force all work into one planning style.

Predictable work can be planned more conventionally.

Exploratory work should be planned around hypotheses, experiments, decision criteria, and time-boxed learning cycles.

This is what allows the project to remain governed without pretending the unknown is already settled.

Learning objectives are a core planning tool

Many AI efforts become inefficient because teams experiment actively but learn passively. They try many things without clearly defining what each experiment is meant to prove.

The AI Project Manager should insist on explicit learning objectives.

A learning objective is not simply "see if this works." It should identify what must be known, why it matters, and what decision it will inform.

Examples include:

- whether existing case data is sufficient to support acceptable classification quality
- whether retrieval grounding materially reduces hallucinated content
- whether human reviewers can validate AI outputs within acceptable effort
- whether the workflow benefits are large enough to justify continued investment
- whether the AI performs consistently enough on high-priority case types to support pilot progression

This approach helps turn experimentation into managed discovery rather than trial-and-error theater.

Exhibit 11A — Planning AI Work Under Uncertainty

Planning Area	Traditional Project Assumption	AI Project Reality	AI PM Response
Scope	Requirements can be defined early and held stable	Feasibility and quality may need to be discovered	Plan around validated scope, not assumed scope
Timeline	Delivery tasks are mostly predictable	Some learning paths are uncertain	Use time-boxed experiments and staged decisions
Success Criteria	Functional completion is the main measure	Quality, trust, and usability must be proven	Define evidence-based success criteria
Risks	Risks are exceptions to the plan	Uncertainty is built into the work	Convert unknowns into learning objectives
Progress	Activity often signals movement	Activity may not prove viability	Measure progress through evidence gained

Decision points must be planned in advance

Uncertain work becomes much safer when the project knows in advance when decisions will be made and what those decisions depend on.

The AI Project Manager should define major decision points such as:

- whether the use case is viable enough to continue
- whether the data is good enough to justify deeper investment
- whether experimentation should narrow scope
- whether pilot readiness has been earned
- whether the business value case still holds

These should not be treated as casual moments of opinion. They should be tied to predefined questions and evidence expectations.

This is important because AI projects often suffer from momentum bias. If the team has already invested significant time and effort, there is pressure to keep going even when the evidence is weak. Planned decision points interrupt that pattern and force the organization to ask whether continued investment is actually justified.

Time-box experimentation without trivializing it

Some organizations respond to AI uncertainty by allowing exploration to continue indefinitely. Others react in the opposite direction and impose rigid deadlines that leave no room for real learning.

The AI Project Manager must balance both extremes.

Experiments should be time-boxed so the project does not drift endlessly. But the time box should be tied to a real learning agenda, not to artificial optimism. The question is not whether the team can "finish AI" in four weeks. The question is whether the team can generate enough credible evidence within a defined period to support the next decision.

That is a more realistic and more useful planning posture.

A completed example — planning an AI document-classification initiative

Consider a team launching an AI initiative to classify incoming compliance documents. The sponsor wants the project delivered quickly, but several uncertainties exist. It is not yet clear whether the historical document set is clean enough, whether the categories are stable, or whether reviewers will trust the classification results.

A weak planning approach would build a full end-to-end schedule immediately and assume the AI will meet quality needs once development begins.

A stronger AI PM approach would separate the plan into two modes.

The first mode covers known work: stakeholder alignment, governance engagement, data access coordination, workflow mapping, and reporting cadence.

The second mode covers uncertain work: a time-boxed experiment to test classification performance against selected categories, a review of label consistency, and a controlled assessment of reviewer effort.

The AI Project Manager defines learning objectives for each experiment, sets a decision point at the end of the exploration window, and makes clear that the project will proceed, narrow scope, or pause based on the evidence gathered.

That is disciplined planning under uncertainty.

What this chapter means for leaders

Leaders should understand that AI uncertainty is not an excuse for weak management. It is the reason stronger management is needed.

The right response to uncertainty is not to demand false precision or to abandon discipline. It is to plan differently: define learning objectives, structure experiments, set decision points, and require evidence before expanding commitment.

That is how AI projects remain accountable without becoming rigid.

Takeaway

AI projects cannot be planned as though all-important answers are known from the start. But they also should not be run as unbounded experimentation. The AI Project Manager must structure uncertainty through explicit learning objectives, time-boxed experiments, predefined decision points, and evidence-based progression. In AI, disciplined planning does not eliminate uncertainty. It makes uncertainty manageable.

Chapter 12

Managing AI Delivery in Phases

Why phased delivery matters in AI

AI projects often fail because organizations try to collapse the lifecycle. They move from idea to build too quickly, from proof-of-concept to production too casually, or from pilot enthusiasm to scale without forcing the evidence required at each step.

A phase-based delivery model helps prevent that.

The point of phasing is not bureaucracy. It is clarity. Each stage should answer a different question, require a different level of proof, and support a different kind of decision. Without that structure, AI projects become confused about what they are actually trying to prove and when they are entitled to move forward.

The AI Project Manager plays a central role here. The role helps ensure that discovery is not mistaken for feasibility, feasibility is not mistaken for pilot readiness, and pilot success is not mistaken for production maturity.

That sequencing is essential in AI because value, quality, and trust are often earned progressively rather than proven all at once.

The stage model for AI delivery

The approved lifecycle in this book is:

discovery, feasibility, proof of concept, pilot, production, and scale.

The AI Project Manager should treat these as decision stages, not simply labels for activity.

Discovery

Discovery clarifies the use case, the business problem, the operating context, and the value hypothesis. The question here is whether this is a worthwhile AI candidate at all.

Feasibility

Feasibility tests whether the conditions exist to continue. This includes data, workflow fit, basic technical plausibility, sponsor commitment, and governance viability.

Proof of Concept

The proof of concept asks whether the core AI approach can perform credibly enough in a controlled setting to justify broader investment.

Pilot

The pilot asks whether the AI works in a real but bounded environment with real users, real process context, and practical operational conditions.

Production

Production asks whether the solution is ready for live operational use with clear ownership, support, governance, and acceptable performance.

Scale

Scale asks whether the solution should be expanded across broader volume, scope, user groups, or business units without losing control or value.

Each phase exists for a reason. The AI Project Manager's job is to keep those reasons clear.

Exhibit 12A — Stage-Based AI Delivery Model

Stage	Main Question	What It Should Prove	AI PM Focus
Discovery	Is this an AI problem worth pursuing?	Business relevance and initial value logic	Clarify problem, sponsor, and scope
Feasibility	Can this use case credibly proceed?	Basic readiness across data, process, and governance	Surface constraints early
Proof of Concept	Can the core approach work?	Technical promise under controlled conditions	Define test boundaries and evidence

Pilot	Can it work in a bounded real environment?	Usability, workflow fit, and practical value	Coordinate live learning with control
Production	Is it ready for sustained live operation?	Ownership, support, stability, and governance readiness	Prepare go-live decision
Scale	Should it be expanded?	Repeatability, supportability, and broader value case	Prevent premature expansion

What evidence belongs in each stage

One of the AI Project Manager's most important responsibilities is making sure the evidence gathered matches the purpose of the stage.

Discovery should produce problem clarity, a defined use case, a value hypothesis, and initial stakeholder alignment.

Feasibility should produce a clearer view of data readiness, process suitability, technical constraints, ownership, and control considerations.

Proof of concept should produce controlled performance evidence. It is not meant to prove full production readiness.

Pilot should produce evidence about real-user behavior, workflow fit, support implications, and practical business value in bounded live conditions.

Production should be supported by evidence that governance, ownership, support, process fit, and technical stability are strong enough for live use.

Scale should require evidence that the capability is repeatable, supportable, and economically sensible at broader reach.

This matters because organizations often ask one stage to answer the wrong question. That is where poor decisions begin.

Proceed, pause, or stop must remain real options

A phased model only works if stages can lead to different decisions.

The AI Project Manager should make it clear that the outcome of a stage is not automatically progression. Sometimes the right answer is to proceed. Sometimes it is to pause for remediation. Sometimes it is to narrow scope. Sometimes it is to stop.

That is not failure. That is disciplined delivery.

AI initiatives create strong pressure to keep moving. But if every phase leads forward regardless of evidence, then the stage model becomes decorative. The AI Project Manager helps preserve its integrity by linking movement to proof.

A completed example — stage-managing an AI service-desk assistant

A company wants to launch an AI assistant for internal service-desk agents.

In discovery, the AI Project Manager helps define the problem: agents spend too much time searching multiple knowledge sources and drafting repetitive responses.

In feasibility, the team confirms that usable knowledge content exists, ownership is clear enough, and governance will permit an advisory use case.

In the proof of concept, the team tests whether grounded AI answers are relevant enough to justify further work.

In the pilot, a limited agent group uses the tool in a real workflow, revealing both benefits and weaknesses in outdated source content.

In production preparation, the AI Project Manager ensures support ownership, content-refresh responsibility, escalation logic, and monitoring are defined.

Only then does the organization make a production decision.

That is how phased delivery prevents the project from skipping maturity steps.

What this chapter means for leaders

Leaders should see phased delivery as a discipline that protects both speed and judgment. It allows the organization to move without pretending that every early signal is enough to justify the next level of commitment.

AI projects should earn the right to advance.

Takeaway

AI delivery should be managed through clear stages: discovery, feasibility, proof of concept, pilot, production, and scale. Each stage exists to answer a different question and gather different evidence. The AI Project Manager helps keep those stages meaningful by ensuring that the project proceeds, pauses, narrows, or stops based on evidence rather than momentum. In AI, phases are not paperwork. They are how disciplined delivery is preserved.

Chapter 13

Human-in-the-Loop Design and Decision Controls

Why human oversight must be designed, not assumed

Many organizations say they want humans in the loop. Far fewer define what that actually means.

In AI delivery, "human-in-the-loop" can quickly become an empty comfort phrase unless the organization answers harder questions. Who reviews what? At what point? Under what threshold? With what authority? What happens when the AI is uncertain? What happens when the human disagrees? Who is accountable for the final outcome?

These questions matter because oversight is only real when it is operationally specific.

The AI Project Manager should treat human-in-the-loop design as a delivery issue, not merely a governance slogan. The role must help the team define where human judgment remains necessary, what control points are needed, and how those controls will function inside the actual workflow.

That is especially important in AI because many failures occur not when the AI acts alone, but when the human-control model is vague, unrealistic, or inconsistently applied.

The AI Project Manager's role in decision controls

The AI Project Manager is not usually the person deciding the detailed risk policy or technical model logic. But the role is central in ensuring that decision controls are designed, documented, tested, and understood.

This includes helping the organization answer:

- which outputs are advisory and which support action
- which cases require human review
- what confidence or risk thresholds change the workflow

- who can approve, override, or reject the AI's recommendation
- how exceptions are handled
- how decisions are logged
- where accountability sits after the human step

These are core project design questions because they shape the operating model, support burden, user training, and governance posture of the AI solution.

Not every use case needs the same human control model

A common mistake is assuming that one oversight model fits all AI use cases.

It does not.

Some AI systems are best used as purely advisory tools where humans review all outputs before acting. Some may support partial automation for low-risk cases while escalating others for human review. Some may allow action within narrow boundaries but require human approval for exceptions. Higher-risk use cases may demand more frequent review, stronger approval logic, or more detailed audit logging.

The AI Project Manager should help ensure that the human-control model matches the use case's risk, impact, workflow, and user capability.

This is not about abstract caution. It is about usable control.

If the oversight model is too weak, the organization takes unacceptable risk.

If it is too heavy, users may bypass it, slow the workflow excessively, or lose the value the AI was meant to create.

Exhibit 13A — Questions That Make Human-in-the-Loop Real

Control Question	Why It Matters	AI PM Concern
What does the AI produce?	Determines the level of downstream risk	Is the output advisory, recommended, or action-triggering?
Which cases require human review?	Prevents blanket or inconsistent control	Are thresholds explicit and usable?
Who can approve or override?	Clarifies accountability in practice	Is authority assigned clearly?
What happens when the AI is uncertain?	Defines safe fallback behavior	Is exception handling built into the workflow?
What is logged?	Supports traceability and governance	Can the organization review decisions later?
How will users be trained?	Prevents misuse and overreliance	Do people know when to trust and when to challenge?

Thresholds matter because vague oversight fails

Human review must not be left to intuition alone.

The AI Project Manager should encourage the team to define thresholds that trigger different control paths. Those thresholds may relate to confidence, case type, risk category, customer impact, monetary value, policy sensitivity, or exception conditions.

The exact mechanism will vary by use case, but the principle is the same: humans need clear rules for when they must review, when they may approve, and when the AI's output is not enough on its own.

Without this clarity, one of two failures usually appears.

Either users over-trust the AI and wave decisions through.

Or users distrust it so much that every output is treated as suspect, destroying the efficiency benefit.

Well-designed thresholds help create practical and proportional oversight.

Exception handling must be part of the design

A human-in-the-loop model is only as credible as its treatment of exceptions.

What happens when the AI output is incomplete, contradictory, or unusually confident in a weak answer? What happens when the case falls outside expected patterns? What happens when a user cannot tell whether the output should be trusted? What happens when the AI recommendation conflicts with policy, expert judgment, or upstream data?

The AI Project Manager should ensure these questions are resolved in the workflow design, not left for users to improvise under pressure.

Exception handling is where oversight becomes operationally real.

Accountability boundaries must remain visible

One of the most important functions of human-in-the-loop design is preserving accountability.

A human review step does not automatically solve accountability if no one is clear about what the human is expected to assess, what the AI was supposed to do, and who ultimately owns the decision.

The AI Project Manager should help make sure the control design distinguishes clearly among:

- AI recommendation responsibility
- human review responsibility
- approval responsibility
- operational accountability
- auditability requirements

This is critical because poorly defined accountability creates a dangerous illusion: everyone assumes a human is "in the loop," yet no one can later explain who was actually responsible for the decision quality.

A completed example — human review design for AI claims routing

An insurer implements AI to recommend routing for incoming claims.

A weak control model would simply say that adjusters can review the AI output if they want.

A stronger AI PM-led design would go further. Standard, low-complexity claims might be auto-routed with later audit sampling. Claims with certain litigation indicators, unusual documentation patterns, or conflicting metadata might require mandatory human review. High-risk claims might require supervisor approval before routing is finalized.

The AI Project Manager helps define those thresholds, clarifies who reviews and who approves, ensures exceptions are logged, and makes sure users are trained to understand when the AI is supportive and when it is not sufficient on its own.

That is what makes human-in-the-loop design real rather than symbolic.

What this chapter means for leaders

Leaders should understand that saying "a human will review it" is not a complete control design. Oversight must be specific enough to function under real operating conditions.

The organization must define thresholds, approvals, exception paths, and accountability boundaries in ways people can actually follow.

That work is part of delivery, not something to be left vague until after launch.

Takeaway

Human-in-the-loop oversight only works when it is designed explicitly. The AI Project Manager helps make that possible by ensuring that review points, thresholds, approvals, overrides, exception handling, and accountability boundaries are defined clearly and integrated into the real workflow. In AI projects, human oversight is not a slogan. It is a control design that must be made operational.

Chapter 14

Change Management and Adoption

Why technically sound AI still fails

Many AI initiatives fail even when the model works reasonably well.

They fail because users do not trust the output. They fail because managers do not change expectations. They fail because training was too shallow. They fail because the workflow around the AI was not redesigned. They fail because people do not understand how the tool should change their decisions, their sequence of work, or their accountability.

In other words, they fail because the organization treated adoption as something secondary.

The AI Project Manager should not make that mistake.

Change management in AI is not a communication add-on at the end of the project. It is part of delivery itself. If people will need to work differently, think differently, escalate differently, or trust differently, that change has to be planned, supported, and reinforced just as deliberately as the technology.

That is what this chapter is about.

The AI Project Manager's role in adoption

The AI Project Manager is not usually the sole owner of enterprise change management, but the role is central to making sure adoption is built into the project rather than bolted on at the end.

This means the AI Project Manager should help ensure that the project addresses:

- who will be affected by the AI
- what will change in their workflow
- what new behaviors are required

- what concerns or resistance are likely
- what communication is needed
- what training is needed
- what managers must reinforce
- how adoption will be measured after rollout

This is especially important in AI because adoption depends on both usability and trust. Users must understand not only how to use the AI, but also when to rely on it, when to question it, and how it affects their role.

That is a more complex change challenge than ordinary tool rollout.

AI adoption is partly behavioral and partly structural

Organizations sometimes treat adoption as a matter of persuasion. They focus heavily on messaging, excitement, and executive sponsorship. Those things help, but they are not enough.

People adopt AI more readily when the environment supports adoption.

That means the workflow must fit.

The human-review model must make sense.

The training must reflect real tasks.

The metrics and incentives must not punish the behaviors the AI requires.

Managers must reinforce the new operating model.

The AI Project Manager should therefore think of adoption as both behavioral and structural. The organization is not simply asking people to like the AI. It is asking them to work differently in a way that must make operational sense.

Exhibit 14A — Core Adoption Questions for AI Projects

Adoption Question	Why It Matters	AI PM Concern
Who is affected?	Different groups experience the AI differently	Have stakeholder groups been mapped properly?
What changes in the workflow?	Adoption fails if the process impact is unclear	Has the future-state workflow been defined?
What new judgment is required?	AI often changes how people review and decide	Are roles and expectations clear?
What concerns will users have?	Trust barriers can block usage even if quality is good	Has resistance been anticipated honestly?
What training is needed?	Users must know both how and when to use AI	Is training practical and scenario-based?
How will adoption be measured?	Launch does not equal uptake	Are post-launch adoption indicators defined?

Trust-building must be practical

Trust in AI is not built by slogans about innovation.

It is built by experience, clarity, and transparency.

Users are more likely to trust AI when:

- the purpose is clear
- the use case is understandable
- the limitations are acknowledged
- the controls are visible
- the outputs are useful in real work
- the escalation path is clear
- leaders do not oversell the AI as infallible

The AI Project Manager should help ensure that trust-building is grounded in the actual operating model. Overstating AI capability often damages adoption more than it helps. Users lose confidence quickly when the messaging sounds stronger than the reality.

Honest trust-building is better than promotional trust-building.

Training must reflect real use, not generic orientation

AI training often fails because it is too abstract. Users are shown what the tool can do, but not how it should be used in the actual workflow. They learn features, but not judgment. They hear optimism, but not limits.

The AI Project Manager should push for scenario-based training that reflects real tasks, real exceptions, real review decisions, and real escalation patterns.

Users should understand:

- what the AI is for
- what it is not for
- what good usage looks like
- when human review is required
- how to challenge weak outputs
- how the workflow changes
- how issues should be reported

That kind of training supports usable adoption rather than superficial awareness.

Workflow redesign is often the hidden adoption issue

Some AI projects fail not because people reject the AI, but because the surrounding process was never properly redesigned.

The AI may generate a recommendation, but no one knows where it fits in the sequence of work. The AI may reduce one manual step while creating two new review steps. The AI may help frontline staff, but upstream and downstream teams may not be ready for the changed flow. Managers may still be measuring performance in ways that reflect the old process.

The AI Project Manager should treat workflow redesign as part of delivery, not as an afterthought.

Adoption depends heavily on whether the AI fits the actual operating model.

Operating-model change must be acknowledged

AI often changes more than task execution. It can also change roles, escalation patterns, review expectations, decision authority, and service ownership.

That means some AI initiatives involve operating-model change, not just tool adoption.

The AI Project Manager should help the organization make that visible early. Otherwise, the project may underestimate the real effort required for adoption. A technically successful project can still stall if no one has thought through how responsibilities, controls, and performance expectations change once the AI is introduced.

A completed example — adoption planning for an AI service-desk copilot

A company introduces an AI copilot for service-desk agents. The tool can summarize tickets, suggest responses, and recommend likely categories.

A weak adoption approach would announce the tool, provide basic training, and assume agents will naturally begin using it.

A stronger AI PM-led approach would map stakeholder groups, identify how agent workflow changes, clarify when suggestions are advisory versus review-worthy, create scenario-based training, prepare managers to reinforce the intended usage model, and define post-launch indicators such as adoption rate, override behavior, user confidence, and rework levels.

The AI Project Manager would also ensure that workflow and performance measures are reviewed so that agents are not penalized for following the new review steps the AI requires.

That is how change management becomes part of delivery rather than post-launch repair.

What this chapter means for leaders

Leaders should understand that adoption is not separate from implementation. If the organization needs people to trust, use, question, review, or escalate AI differently, then change management is part of the project itself.

That means communication, training, workflow redesign, trust-building, and manager reinforcement must be planned early enough to matter.

Takeaway

Many AI initiatives fail not because the technology is unusable, but because the organization did not prepare people and workflows to work with it. The AI Project Manager helps prevent that by embedding change management into delivery: mapping stakeholders, redesigning workflows, planning training, building trust realistically, and defining how adoption will be measured after launch. In AI, adoption is not a side activity. It is part of whether the project succeeds at all.

Chapter 15

From Pilot to Production

Why this is where many AI projects stall

Many AI initiatives do not fail in discovery.

They do not fail in the proof-of-concept demo.

They do not even fail in the pilot.

They fail in the transition between pilot and production.

This is one of the most painful points in the AI lifecycle because the organization is often close enough to success to feel optimistic, but not mature enough to go live safely at scale. The pilot may have shown promise. Users may like the concept. Executives may already be talking about rollout. Technical teams may feel they have proven the model works "well enough." Yet when the question becomes whether the solution is truly ready for production, uncertainty returns.

That is because pilot success and production readiness are not the same thing.

A pilot can prove that an AI use case is possible. Production must prove that it is governable, supportable, stable, usable, and worth standing behind operationally.

This is where AI project management becomes especially important. The AI Project Manager must help the organization move beyond enthusiasm and ask a harder question: what must be true before this AI solution deserves to operate in the real business environment?

That is the purpose of this chapter.

The AI Project Manager's role in the pilot-to-production transition

At this stage, the AI Project Manager is not simply coordinating a deployment plan. The role becomes the integrator of readiness across business, technical, operational, governance, and adoption dimensions.

This matters because pilot-to-production failure often happens when one group mistakes its own readiness for enterprise readiness. The technical team may believe the solution is ready because performance looks acceptable. The business sponsor may believe it is ready because the use case is exciting. Users may believe it is ready because the pilot helped them. But production requires all readiness conditions to hold together at once.

The AI Project Manager helps test that convergence.

In practical terms, the AI Project Manager should help answer six questions:

Is governance ready for production use?

Is there a clear operational owner after go-live?

Does the AI fit the real business process, not just the pilot scenario?

Is the technical solution stable enough for live use?

Is there a credible support model?

Do the relevant stakeholders have enough confidence to trust the solution in production?

Those are not technical questions alone. They are production transition questions. And they sit squarely in the AI PM domain.

Pilot success is evidence, not permission

One of the most dangerous assumptions in AI delivery is that a successful pilot automatically justifies production rollout.

It does not.

A pilot is designed to learn under bounded conditions. It usually has narrower scope, closer supervision, more tolerant users, more direct involvement from specialists, and more flexibility to absorb imperfection. Production is different. Production means the AI is being asked to function inside a real operating environment where consistency, accountability, support, and trust matter every day.

That is why pilot results should be treated as evidence for a decision, not as automatic permission to proceed.

The AI Project Manager should help frame the transition clearly: the pilot did not answer whether the AI is good in principle; it answered whether the AI is promising enough to evaluate for production readiness.

That distinction protects the organization from scaling optimism instead of scaling evidence.

What must be true before moving beyond pilot mode

The move to production should not depend on one headline metric or one enthusiastic sponsor. It should depend on a set of readiness conditions that together indicate that the solution can survive contact with real operations.

These conditions usually fall into six categories.

1. Governance readiness

The first condition is governance readiness. The organization must know who has approved the solution, under what conditions, within what operating boundaries, and with what escalation path if performance degrades.

This includes decision rights, risk acceptance, control expectations, auditability, and clear go-live authority. If governance is still vague, the solution is not production-ready.

2. Operational ownership

The second condition is operational ownership. Someone in the business must own the live service after go-live. That means ownership of performance, user experience, issue handling, operating decisions, and value realization.

If the AI still feels like "the project team's system," it is probably not ready for production.

3. Process fit

The third condition is process fit. The AI must fit the real workflow, not merely a demonstration workflow or a pilot-safe subset of work. This includes handoffs, exception handling, human review points, turnaround expectations, and interaction with surrounding systems and policies.

An AI that works in isolation but creates friction inside the real process is not ready.

4. Technical stability

The fourth condition is technical stability. This does not mean perfection. It means the solution performs consistently enough, with known limitations, reliable integrations, acceptable latency, stable outputs, and manageable failure behavior for the intended production scope.

A technically interesting pilot is not the same as a stable operational capability.

5. Support capability

The fifth condition is support capability. Production means something happens when the AI behaves poorly, produces bad outputs, fails to retrieve the right information, slows down, confuses users, or requires tuning. If there is no support model, then there is no production model.

6. Stakeholder confidence

The sixth condition is stakeholder confidence. This includes sponsor confidence, operator confidence, user confidence, and risk confidence. Confidence should not be blind optimism. It should be informed confidence based on evidence, known limits, and clear human-control mechanisms.

Without enough confidence, rollout may happen formally but fail behaviorally.

Exhibit 15A — Pilot-to-Production Readiness Conditions

Readiness Area	Key Question	Why It Matters	AI PM Concern
Governance Readiness	Has the AI been approved with clear operating boundaries and escalation paths?	Prevents uncontrolled go-live	Is the decision framework complete?
Operational Ownership	Who owns the AI after launch?	Prevents orphaned production services	Has a real owner accepted accountability?
Process Fit	Does the AI fit the live workflow, including exceptions?	Avoids operational friction and rework	Has the end-to-end process been tested realistically?
Technical Stability	Is the AI stable enough for intended production scope?	Reduces unpredictable live behavior	Are known limits explicit and acceptable?
Support Capability	Can the organization support, fix, and monitor the AI?	Prevents fragile go-live	Is there a credible support model?
Stakeholder Confidence	Do business, users, and governance stakeholders trust the production model?	Supports adoption and controlled use	Is confidence evidence-based or only emotional?

Governance readiness is more than a signoff

Many organizations treat governance as a final approval event. In reality, governance readiness is about whether the enterprise knows how the AI will be controlled in production.

That includes questions such as:

- What decisions can the AI influence or automate?
- What level of human review is required?
- What outputs are considered advisory versus actionable?

- What risk controls must remain in place after launch?
- What incidents require escalation?
- What changes can be made without formal reapproval?
- What performance decline would trigger review or rollback?

The AI Project Manager should ensure that these questions are answered before production, not discovered afterward in confusion.

A pilot can tolerate some governance ambiguity because exposure is bounded. Production cannot.

Operational ownership is one of the clearest dividing lines

A surprising number of AI initiatives reach the edge of rollout without a true operational owner.

The sponsor supported the pilot.

The project team managed the work.

The technical team tuned the solution.

Users participated in testing.

But when the question becomes who owns the AI on a Tuesday morning three months after launch, the answer becomes unclear.

That is a red flag.

The AI Project Manager should press for explicit operational ownership before production approval. Someone must own live performance, business fit, issue triage, escalation decisions, user feedback patterns, and ongoing value tracking. Without this, the organization has built a prototype with no enduring home.

Production is not just a technical state. It is an ownership state.

Process fit is where many promising pilots break down

A pilot often operates in a cleaner environment than production. Cases may be selected carefully. Users may be more attentive. Exceptions may be handled manually without much concern. Edge cases may be excluded. Workflow disruptions may be tolerated because the pilot is temporary.

Production removes those protections.

That is why the AI Project Manager should insist on testing for real process fit. The questions are practical:

- Does the AI fit the actual sequence of work?
- Can people understand when to rely on it and when to intervene?
- What happens when the AI is uncertain?
- What happens when upstream data is incomplete?
- What happens when the case does not match expected patterns?
- Does the AI save steps or create hidden rework?
- Are surrounding teams prepared for the changed workflow?

An AI solution that performs well in a bounded pilot but degrades the real process is not ready for production, even if the model itself seems strong.

Technical stability must be sufficient for the approved scope

In AI projects, technical teams are often asked whether the solution is ready. The more useful question is whether the solution is stable enough for the intended production scope.

That wording matters.

Many AI systems are not uniformly reliable across all tasks, cases, or conditions. They may be strong in common cases and weaker in edge cases. They may be stable in one business unit and less stable in another. They may perform differently when connected to live sources than when evaluated on test data. They may work acceptably with human review but not safely in higher-autonomy settings.

The AI Project Manager should therefore help frame technical readiness in scoped terms:

- stable enough for what kinds of cases?
- stable enough under what volume?
- stable enough with what human controls?
- stable enough with what fallback path?
- stable enough with what support response?

This helps prevent the false binary of "ready" versus "not ready" and instead supports controlled production decisions based on evidence.

Support capability is part of the launch decision

One of the most common pilot traps is assuming that because the project team can support the AI during the pilot, the organization has a support model for production.

Those are not the same thing.

Pilots often rely on unusually high-touch support. Engineers monitor behavior closely. The project team responds rapidly to issues. Business users tolerate imperfections because the effort is still experimental. This can make support look easier than it really is.

The AI Project Manager should force the production question: who will support this when it is no longer a special project?

That includes:

- first-line issue intake
- technical triage
- business escalation

- model or prompt adjustment ownership
- retrieval/content refresh responsibility
- incident classification
- rollback or containment authority
- user communication when something changes

If the answers depend on temporary pilot arrangements, the solution is not yet production-ready.

Stakeholder confidence must be earned, not assumed

Confidence is often misunderstood in AI delivery. It is sometimes treated as a soft feeling, secondary to technical performance. But production rollout depends on confidence in a very practical sense.

Users must trust the AI enough to use it properly.

Managers must trust it enough to include it in performance expectations.

Risk teams must trust the controls enough to allow live operation.

Operations leaders must trust the support model enough to accept ownership.

Sponsors must trust the value case enough to defend continued investment.

The AI Project Manager should assess confidence carefully. Too little confidence leads to rejection, workarounds, and low adoption. Too much confidence leads to overreliance, unsafe shortcuts, and ignored controls.

Healthy production confidence comes from transparent evidence, clear boundaries, visible human override mechanisms, and honest communication about limitations.

Exhibit 15B — Common Reasons AI Projects Stall Between Pilot and Production

Stall Point	What It Usually Means	AI PM Response
"The pilot worked, but leadership is hesitating"	Production readiness is not fully proven	Reframe discussion around readiness conditions, not pilot success alone
"No one wants to own it after launch"	Operational ownership is unresolved	Escalate ownership as a formal gate issue
"Users liked it, but process teams are nervous"	Workflow fit is incomplete	Validate end-to-end process implications more deeply
"The model is good enough, but support is unclear"	Technical viability exists without operating capability	Build and approve a real support model
"Governance still has questions"	Risk/control boundaries are unresolved	Convert open concerns into explicit launch criteria
"We want to scale, but edge cases remain weak"	Scope is too broad for current maturity	Recommend constrained production rather than broad rollout

The transition decision should be structured, not emotional

The move from pilot to production should be treated as a stage-gate decision, not a momentum event.

Momentum is dangerous here because pilot success often creates pressure. Sponsors want results. Teams want recognition for progress. Executives want visible wins. Vendors may encourage acceleration. But production decisions made from momentum rather than readiness often create setbacks that damage trust far more than a disciplined delay would have.

The AI Project Manager should therefore structure the transition around explicit decision options:

- proceed to production
- proceed to constrained production

- extend pilot
- remediate and re-evaluate
- pause or re-scope

This framing is important because it turns the conversation away from "Are we brave enough to launch?" and toward "Which decision best matches the evidence we have?"

That is how enterprise AI delivery stays disciplined under pressure.

Constrained production is often the smartest bridge

Organizations sometimes act as though there are only two options: stay in pilot or go fully live. In many cases, the right answer is a controlled middle step.

Constrained production can be an effective bridge when the AI has earned partial trust but not broad production scope. For example, the organization may launch:

- for specific case types only
- with mandatory human review
- in one business unit only
- with capped transaction volume
- with restricted automation authority
- with additional monitoring for a defined period

This is often where the AI Project Manager adds real value. The role can help prevent the false choice between overcautious stagnation and overconfident rollout.

A disciplined constrained production model lets the organization keep learning in a real environment while preserving control.

Exhibit 15C — Production Decision Paths

Decision Path	When It Fits	Benefit	Risk
Full Production	Readiness is strong across governance, ownership, process, stability, support, and confidence	Fastest route to value realization	Greater exposure if readiness was overstated
Constrained Production	Core value is proven, but some boundaries still need control	Balanced path between learning and control	May create pressure to scale prematurely
Extended Pilot	Important evidence is still missing	More learning before exposure expands	Pilot fatigue and unclear momentum
Remediate and Re-Evaluate	Specific weaknesses are known and fixable	Focused correction before rollout	Delay may frustrate sponsors
Pause or Re-Scope	Use case is not production-ready in current form	Prevents scaling the wrong solution	Can be politically difficult

What the AI Project Manager should bring to the production decision

By the time a project reaches this stage, the AI Project Manager should be able to present a production-readiness view that is more useful than a generic status report.

That view should include:

- what the pilot actually proved
- what it did not prove
- what readiness conditions are met
- which gaps remain open
- the risks of proceeding now
- the risks of delaying

- the proposed production scope
- the support and ownership model
- the recommended decision path

This is where the AI PM role becomes especially enterprise-relevant. The quality of the decision often depends on whether someone has integrated evidence across business, technical, governance, adoption, and operational dimensions.

That is not a side task. It is one of the most valuable contributions of AI project management.

A completed example — moving an AI claims summarization pilot into production

Consider an insurer that piloted an AI claims summarization tool for adjusters. During the pilot, the tool reduced time spent reviewing long claim files and improved adjuster satisfaction. Pilot users reported that the summaries helped them get oriented faster and identify likely next steps more efficiently.

On the surface, this looked like a success. The sponsor wanted enterprise rollout.

But the AI Project Manager organized the production review around the six readiness conditions rather than the positive pilot sentiment alone.

Governance readiness was partially complete. The solution had acceptable controls for standard claim summaries, but there was still uncertainty around how summaries should be used in higher-risk claim situations involving legal disputes.

Operational ownership was strong. Claims operations was willing to own the live service.

Process fit was mostly positive, but only for standard workflows. The tool had not yet been fully integrated into the edge-case review process.

Technical stability was acceptable for common claims but less reliable on unusually complex file structures.

Support capability existed, but was still too dependent on the project team for rapid fixes.

Stakeholder confidence was high among pilot users, moderate among operations leaders, and cautious among risk stakeholders.

Based on this, the AI Project Manager did not recommend a full enterprise rollout. Instead, the recommendation was constrained production: go live for defined claim categories, require human review in high-risk cases, formalize the support model, and revisit broader rollout after a defined production observation period.

Leadership approved that path.

The result was that the project did move forward, but it moved forward in a way that matched the evidence. The organization did not mistake pilot enthusiasm for production proof.

That is what disciplined AI project management looks like at the transition point.

Production readiness is also a trust decision

This chapter has focused on readiness, but beneath all of it is a broader issue: trust.

Production means the organization is willing to place the AI inside real work, real decisions, real customer interactions, or real operational flows. That is an institutional trust act. It should never be casual.

The AI Project Manager helps make that trust deserved rather than assumed.

By forcing clarity on governance, ownership, process fit, stability, support, and confidence, the AI PM helps ensure that go-live is not a leap of faith. It becomes a governed decision made with open eyes.

That is one of the deepest differences between AI project management and ordinary deployment coordination.

What this chapter means for leaders

Leaders should leave this chapter with one central understanding: a pilot is not a near-production form of success. It is a learning stage. Production must be earned separately.

That means the decision to move forward should not be driven by excitement, sunk cost, or pressure to show momentum. It should be driven by readiness across governance, operational ownership, process fit, technical stability, support capability, and stakeholder confidence.

The AI Project Manager plays a central role in making that judgment possible by integrating these factors into a decision-ready view.

Takeaway

The move from pilot to production is one of the most fragile and important transitions in the AI lifecycle. Many efforts stall here because pilot promise is mistaken for operational readiness. A production-worthy AI solution must show not only useful results, but also governance readiness, operational ownership, process fit, technical stability, support capability, and stakeholder confidence.

The AI Project Manager is critical at this stage because the role helps the organization distinguish between what the pilot proved and what production still requires.

In AI, the question is not whether the pilot worked.

The question is whether the organization is truly ready to live with the AI in production.

Chapter 16

Monitoring, Drift, and Continuous Improvement

Why launch is not the end of the AI project

Many organizations still treat launch as the finish line.

The project is declared complete. The steering group turns its attention elsewhere. The business assumes the value will now flow. The technical team moves on to the next priority. Support is told to "keep an eye on it." At that point, the organization often believes the hard part is over.

In AI, the opposite is often true.

Launch is the moment when the AI solution leaves the relative safety of controlled testing, bounded pilots, and intensified project attention. It enters the messiness of real business conditions, live user behavior, changing data, operational exceptions, process shifts, content changes, model updates, and rising stakeholder expectations. That is where weak assumptions become visible. That is where value claims are tested against reality. That is where confidence can either deepen or collapse.

This is why post-launch management is not a side activity. It is part of the AI project itself.

The AI Project Manager should not treat go-live as the point where responsibility disappears. Instead, the role should help ensure that the organization has a disciplined model for monitoring performance, identifying drift, responding to incidents, managing updates, and improving the AI without destabilizing the live service.

A launched AI system is not a completed object. It is a managed capability.

The AI Project Manager's role after launch

After launch, the AI Project Manager is no longer managing a pilot or preparing for production. The role shifts into post-launch governance and control.

This does not mean the AI Project Manager becomes the operational owner, support analyst, model engineer, or platform administrator. But it does mean the AI Project

Manager plays a central role in making sure the organization knows how the AI will be watched, how changes will be judged, when issues will be escalated, and how improvement will occur without becoming chaos.

In practice, the AI Project Manager should help ensure five things.

First, that the organization is monitoring the right things, not just technical uptime.

Second, that drift is recognized as a management issue, not merely a technical curiosity.

Third, that incidents involving AI behavior are identified and handled with a structured response model.

Fourth, that changes to prompts, models, data sources, thresholds, or workflows are treated as governed changes rather than casual tuning.

Fifth, that continuous improvement remains tied to business value, user trust, and control boundaries.

This is where AI project management extends into operational discipline.

Monitoring must go beyond technical availability

Traditional post-launch monitoring often begins with system availability, latency, and error rates. Those still matter in AI, but they are not enough.

An AI service can be technically available and still be operationally failing.

It may be producing lower-quality outputs. It may be retrieving stale or irrelevant information. It may be confusing users. It may be creating more human rework than expected. It may be increasing override rates. It may be drifting away from the workflow it was designed to support. It may be gradually losing the trust of the people who are supposed to use it.

That is why AI monitoring must include broader categories of evidence.

The AI Project Manager should ensure the organization monitors across at least five dimensions:

- business value and service impact

- output quality and reliability
- usage and human behavior
- risk and control performance
- technical and operational stability

Without this broader lens, the organization may think the AI is healthy simply because the platform is running.

Exhibit 16A — What Should Be Monitored After Launch

Monitoring Area	Key Question	Example Indicators	AI PM Concern
Business Value	Is the AI still producing the intended business outcome?	cycle time, productivity gain, deflection rate, cost avoidance, SLA improvement	Is the value case holding in real operations?
Output Quality	Are the outputs still reliable enough for use?	accuracy, relevance, review-pass rate, rework rate, exception rate	Is quality staying within approved limits?
Usage and Behavior	Are users relying on the AI appropriately?	adoption rate, override rate, fallback rate, abandonment rate	Is trust strengthening or weakening?
Risk and Control	Is the AI operating within governance boundaries?	harmful-output rate, policy exceptions, complaint volume, audit gaps	Are control assumptions still valid?
Technical Stability	Is the live service operating consistently?	latency, downtime, integration failures, queue backlogs	Is technical instability undermining business use?

Drift is one of the most important post-launch realities

One of the defining characteristics of AI systems is that acceptable performance at one point in time does not guarantee acceptable performance later.

That is why drift matters so much.

Drift simply means that the conditions under which the AI was validated are no longer fully aligned with the conditions under which it is operating. Sometimes that change is obvious. Often it is gradual.

The AI Project Manager does not need to be the person diagnosing the technical mechanics of drift. But the AI Project Manager must make sure the organization is prepared to notice it, interpret it, and act on it.

That is a management responsibility.

Too many organizations treat drift as something the technical team will "handle if it happens." That is not a strategy. Drift needs defined indicators, review ownership, escalation thresholds, and decision paths.

Otherwise, performance can deteriorate in slow motion while everyone assumes the AI is still behaving as approved.

Different kinds of drift matter in different ways

In AI project management, it is useful to think of drift broadly rather than only as model drift.

Several kinds of drift can undermine a live AI service.

1. Data drift

The incoming data changes. Fields shift. formats evolve. volumes change. categories expand. input quality declines. Upstream systems begin feeding information differently than before.

2. Prompt or instruction drift

Over time, prompts, system instructions, guardrails, or business rules may be adjusted in ways that subtly alter the AI's behavior. This may happen intentionally or gradually through accumulated changes.

3. Retrieval or knowledge drift

For retrieval-based and knowledge-grounded systems, the underlying content may become stale, contradictory, incomplete, or misaligned with current business policy and operating reality.

4. Process drift

The business process around the AI changes. Routing rules change. approval thresholds change. operating teams reorganize. escalation paths move. What once fit the workflow may no longer fit it.

5. User-behavior drift

Users change how they interact with the AI. They may over-rely on it, underuse it, bypass it, use it for unsupported tasks, or apply its outputs in ways the original design did not anticipate.

These forms of drift matter because they affect production trust and value. The AI Project Manager should make sure the enterprise is not watching only the model while missing the broader operating environment.

Exhibit 16B — Practical Drift Categories for AI Project Management

Drift Type	What Changes	Likely Effect	AI PM Response
Data Drift	Inputs, labels, formats, or data quality shift	Lower consistency or weaker output quality	Ensure drift indicators, ownership, and review cadence exist
Prompt / Instruction Drift	Prompt logic or rules change over time	Behavior becomes less predictable or less aligned	Require change control for prompt and rule updates
Retrieval / Knowledge Drift	Sources become stale, conflicting, or incomplete	More misinformation or weaker grounding	Define source refresh responsibility and review cycles
Process Drift	Workflow, policy, or operating context changes	AI no longer fits the real business process	Reassess workflow fit and control design
User-Behavior Drift	People change how they use the AI	Overtrust, misuse, low adoption, or hidden workarounds	Review adoption patterns and retrain or redesign as needed

Drift is not only a technical issue. It is a governance issue.

A weak post-launch organization waits until performance failure is obvious.

A disciplined post-launch organization defines what kinds of drift matter, how they will be detected, when they will be reviewed, and what decisions follow if thresholds are breached.

That is why drift should be governed.

The AI Project Manager should help ensure that the organization has clear answers to questions such as:

- What indicators are used to detect drift?
- Who reviews them, and how often?
- What thresholds trigger concern?
- What requires remediation versus escalation?
- What changes require revalidation?
- At what point should production scope be restricted?

These questions are essential because drift is not just about whether the AI is still "smart enough." It is about whether the AI is still operating within the conditions under which the enterprise agreed to trust it.

AI incidents often look different from ordinary IT incidents

Not every AI problem looks like a traditional outage.

Sometimes the system is up, the integrations are working, and response times are normal, yet the AI is still causing damage. It may be generating poor recommendations, surfacing false content, producing inconsistent summaries, failing silently on important edge cases, or creating a surge in human overrides and complaints.

That means incident thinking must expand.

An AI incident is not only a platform failure. It is any material event in which the AI no longer performs within acceptable quality, control, compliance, or operational boundaries.

This distinction is important because ordinary IT incident models may miss or minimize AI-specific failures. The business may experience them first, long before infrastructure dashboards do.

The AI Project Manager should help ensure that the incident model for a live AI capability reflects the actual ways AI can fail.

What a sound AI incident response model should include

The AI Project Manager should help put a practical incident structure in place before serious issues arise.

That structure should typically include:

- clear incident definitions for AI-related failures
- severity levels appropriate to business impact
- containment options such as rollback, human-review mode, or narrowed scope
- assigned owners for triage and root-cause analysis
- evidence capture requirements
- stakeholder communication paths
- post-incident review and corrective action tracking

This matters because AI incidents can tempt teams into informal fixes. A prompt gets adjusted. A source is swapped. A threshold is lowered. A silent correction is made in production. That may solve the symptom, but it often weakens traceability and makes future governance harder.

The AI Project Manager helps prevent this by insisting that correction also remain governable.

Exhibit 16C — AI Incident Types and Management Implications

Incident Type	Example	Business Risk	AI PM Concern
Quality Failure	Sudden decline in summarization or recommendation quality	Wrong decisions, rework, loss of trust	Has the issue been classified and contained?
Retrieval Failure	AI cites stale or irrelevant source material	Misinformation, policy errors, poor decisions	Are source and content owners engaged?
Control Failure	AI exceeds intended authority or bypasses review	Compliance and governance exposure	Are boundaries and escalation paths clear?
User-Behavior Failure	Users over trust, misuse, or bypass the AI	Unsafe operation or low realized value	Does response include change and training actions?
Technical Failure	Latency, outages, broken integrations, queue backlogs	Service interruption and adoption decline	Is the technical issue affecting business acceptability?

Continuous improvement must not become uncontrolled experimentation

Once the AI is live, requests for change usually accelerate.

Users want better outputs. Sponsors want broader scope. Operations wants less manual review. Technical teams want to refine prompts or replace models. Vendors release new capabilities. Business policies change. New data sources become available.

All of this creates pressure to "keep improving."

That is sensible in principle. But without discipline, continuous improvement becomes live experimentation without adequate control.

The AI Project Manager should therefore help separate improvement from improvisation.

Post-launch improvement should be governed by questions such as:

- What problem is the proposed change solving?
- Is the expected benefit clear and measurable?
- Does the change alter the risk profile?
- Does it require new validation?
- Does it affect human review, approval boundaries, or workflow fit?
- Does it change the business case or operating assumptions?
- Who approves it?

These questions keep the organization from treating a live AI service as a playground.

Updating, retraining, and replacement should be treated as decision events

A common mistake in AI operations is to treat updates as inherently positive. A better model appears. A vendor changes capabilities. A new prompt seems to perform better. A retraining opportunity emerges. A fresh content set becomes available.

The organization then assumes it should simply update and move on.

That is not always wise.

Some changes are minor. Others alter the production behavior of the AI enough that they should be treated as formal decision events.

The AI Project Manager should help make sure the enterprise distinguishes among:

- minor tuning changes
- material behavior changes
- model-version changes
- source-content refreshes with governance impact
- retraining events
- decisions to replace or retire the capability

This matters because "improvement" can also mean new instability, new governance exposure, new user confusion, or a broken value case.

The AI PM role helps ensure that the desire to improve does not outrun the discipline to evaluate.

When revalidation should be expected

Not every post-launch change requires the same level of scrutiny. But some changes clearly require revalidation before or during rollout.

Examples include:

- major prompt or instruction changes
- model replacement or version changes
- changes in workflow authority
- new data or knowledge sources
- expansion into new case types or user groups
- control-boundary changes
- changes resulting from a significant incident
- retraining based on materially different data conditions

The AI Project Manager should help define what counts as a revalidation trigger and ensure this is known in advance. Otherwise, teams may make changes that seem operationally convenient but weaken the integrity of the original production approval.

Exhibit 16D — Examples of Post-Launch Change Types

Change Type	Example	Typical Governance Need	AI PM Focus
Minor Tuning	Small wording refinement in a prompt	Light review	Ensure traceability and confirm no material behavior shift
Material Behavior Change	Prompt redesign that changes how outputs are framed or prioritized	Formal review and targeted revalidation	Determine whether operating assumptions changed
Model Change	Vendor model upgrade or replacement	Formal approval and broader revalidation	Protect stability, trust, and comparability
Source / Content Change	New policy corpus or refreshed knowledge base	Review of content ownership and retrieval quality	Ensure grounding quality and source accountability
Scope Expansion	Extending the AI to new case types or business units	Stage-gate style review	Confirm readiness, controls, and supportability
Replacement / Retirement	Replacing the AI or withdrawing it from service	Executive and operational decision	Preserve continuity and value logic

Continuous improvement should be tied to value, not motion

Some post-launch organizations become very active but not very effective. They make frequent changes, run many reviews, and keep a busy backlog of improvement ideas. Yet they lose sight of the core question: is the AI becoming more valuable, more reliable, and more governable over time?

The AI Project Manager should keep the organization anchored to that question.

Continuous improvement should not mean endless activity. It should mean disciplined improvement against the business and operational outcomes that justified the AI in the first place.

That includes asking:

- Is value improving or eroding?
- Is quality becoming more stable?
- Are users gaining trust or losing it?
- Are controls remaining effective?
- Is the support burden rising or falling?
- Is the AI becoming more sustainable to operate?

Improvement without value discipline is just motion.

Review cadence matters

One reason post-launch control weakens is that the organization assumes monitoring can happen passively. In reality, a live AI service needs structured review rhythms.

The AI Project Manager should help ensure that the organization defines review cadences such as:

- frequent operational review in early production
- periodic quality and drift review
- regular stakeholder review of incidents and corrective actions
- scheduled value realization review
- periodic governance review for major or higher-risk services

The precise cadence will vary by use case and risk level. But the principle is consistent: post-launch AI should be reviewed deliberately, not only when something goes wrong.

This turns monitoring from passive observation into active management.

A completed example — managing drift and improvement in a live AI ticket triage service

Consider a live AI ticket triage service used to classify and route internal support tickets.

During the first two months after launch, performance appeared strong. Routing accuracy improved, manual triage effort fell, and service desk supervisors reported early confidence in the tool.

By month three, however, several subtle changes appeared. A new category of access-related requests entered the workflow. A policy update altered the priority logic for certain tickets. At the same time, users began relying on the AI more heavily and were overriding its recommendations less often than during the pilot.

None of these changes looked dramatic in isolation. The service was still available. Overall volume was manageable. No major outage occurred.

But the monitoring model designed during delivery included more than uptime. The weekly review showed a rising error rate in the new access-request category, a mild increase in escalations, and a growing mismatch between AI-recommended priority and the new business rules.

Because the organization had defined drift review ownership and a post-launch governance cadence, the issue did not remain invisible.

The AI Project Manager coordinated the response across the business owner, AI Technical Lead, data and policy stakeholders, and operations lead. The decision was not to leave the service untouched or to make an undocumented quick fix. Instead, the organization classified the issue as a production drift event, temporarily required added human review for the affected category, updated the rules and prompt logic, refreshed the evaluation set, and ran targeted revalidation before returning to normal operating scope.

At the same time, user guidance was reinforced because reduced override behavior suggested rising overreliance. The review therefore treated the issue not just as a technical correction, but also as a human-control issue.

This is what good post-launch AI project management looks like. The AI had not "failed" in the simplistic sense. The operating environment had changed, and the organization was prepared to respond with structure rather than confusion.

The most mature organizations know when improvement is not enough

Some AI services should be improved. Others should be constrained, replaced, or eventually retired.

This is an important post-launch leadership discipline.

The AI Project Manager should help ensure that continuous improvement does not become a refusal to face hard truths. If the AI remains economically weak, operationally unstable, poorly trusted, or too expensive to govern relative to the value it creates, the organization may need to redesign or replace it rather than keep tuning it indefinitely.

This does not mean post-launch management should be pessimistic. It means it should be honest.

Not every live AI capability deserves permanent life. Some deserve disciplined improvement. Some deserve narrower use. Some deserve replacement. A few deserve closure.

The AI PM role helps make that judgment visible before sunk-cost thinking takes over.

What this chapter means for leaders

Leaders should leave this chapter with one central understanding: launch does not end AI project management. It begins a new phase of accountability.

A live AI capability must be monitored for value, quality, use, risk, and stability. Drift must be anticipated, not treated as a surprise. Incidents must be handled in ways that preserve traceability and decision quality. Improvements must be governed so production does not become uncontrolled experimentation. Updates, retraining, replacement, and retirement decisions must be made with evidence.

The AI Project Manager is important here because the role helps ensure that post-launch control is structured, cross-functional, and tied back to the value and trust logic that justified the project in the first place.

Takeaway

AI systems do not remain production-worthy automatically. After launch, they must be monitored, reviewed, corrected, and improved within a disciplined operating model. Drift can emerge through data changes, prompt changes, content changes, process changes, or user-behavior changes. Incidents may appear as quality and control failures even when the technology is still available. Continuous improvement is necessary, but it must be governed carefully so that change does not undermine stability and trust.

The AI Project Manager plays a central role in this phase by helping the enterprise define what to monitor, what counts as drift, how incidents are handled, when revalidation is required, and how improvement remains tied to business value and control.

In AI, going live is not the end of the project.

It is the beginning of managed accountability.

Chapter 17

Measuring ROI and Business Impact

Why AI value must be proven, not presumed

Many AI initiatives sound valuable long before they become valuable.

The use case is attractive. The demo is impressive. The pilot produces enthusiasm. Users say the tool feels helpful. Leaders begin talking about scale. But none of those things, by themselves, prove business impact.

This is one of the most important disciplines in AI project management. AI programs are especially vulnerable to inflated expectations because they often combine strategic excitement, technical novelty, and strong executive attention. That makes it dangerously easy to confuse activity with value, adoption with impact, and promise with return.

The AI Project Manager should not allow the project to stop at optimism.

The real question is not whether the AI was launched, whether the pilot participants liked it, or whether the output looked impressive in a steering meeting. The real question is whether the initiative delivered measurable business benefit in the operating environment for which it was funded.

That is what this chapter addresses.

AI project management is not only about moving an AI capability into production. It is also about helping the organization determine whether the capability created enough value to justify the cost, effort, governance burden, change burden, and operational ownership it required. That means measuring ROI and business impact with discipline.

The AI Project Manager's role in value measurement

The AI Project Manager is not usually the finance owner or the executive accountable for enterprise value realization. But the role is central in making sure value can actually be measured.

That work begins well before launch.

The AI Project Manager should help ensure that the project starts with a defined baseline, a credible value hypothesis, measurable target outcomes, explicit assumptions, and a realistic way to gather post-launch evidence. If those elements are weak during the business-case stage, value measurement later becomes vague, contested, or reduced to narrative.

After launch, the AI Project Manager helps connect projected value to realized value by coordinating the evidence needed to answer questions such as:

- Did the AI improve the business outcome it was supposed to improve?
- Were the savings or gains real, or merely perceived?
- Did hidden support, governance, review, or maintenance costs reduce the return?
- Did value appear consistently, or only under limited conditions?
- Is the benefit durable enough to justify expansion or continued investment?

These are not just reporting questions. They are decision questions. They influence whether the AI should be scaled, narrowed, improved, re-scoped, or stopped.

That is why ROI measurement belongs inside the AI PM discipline rather than being treated as a finance exercise at the end.

Vanity metrics are not business impact

One of the biggest traps in AI programs is measuring what is easy instead of what is meaningful.

It is easy to count prompts submitted, outputs generated, users enrolled, sessions launched, tickets touched, or pilot participation. These numbers may help describe system activity, but they do not necessarily prove business value.

The AI Project Manager should help the organization distinguish clearly between operational signals and business impact.

A high usage rate does not prove the AI saves time.

Positive user feedback does not prove the AI improves quality.

A lower manual task count does not prove end-to-end cycle time improved.

A large volume of generated outputs does not prove those outputs were useful.

Adoption does not prove ROI.

These measures still matter. They help explain what is happening. But they are not enough. AI projects should ultimately be judged on the business outcomes they were meant to influence.

Business impact begins with the original use case logic

Strong value measurement depends on whether the use case was framed properly in the first place.

If the project began with a vague goal such as "improve efficiency" or "use AI to modernize operations," then post-launch ROI analysis will remain fuzzy. But if the use case was built around a concrete operating problem, value measurement becomes far more credible.

For example, stronger value hypotheses sound like this:

- reduce average handling time for claims intake by 20 percent
- improve ticket-routing accuracy from 65 percent to 85 percent
- reduce time spent searching internal policy content by 30 percent
- reduce repeat case handling caused by poor knowledge access
- improve first-response time in a defined support queue
- increase throughput without proportional headcount growth

The AI Project Manager should keep this original value logic visible throughout the lifecycle. Without it, organizations often try to prove value after the fact using whatever metrics happen to be available.

That is not disciplined project management. That is retroactive storytelling.

Exhibit 17A — Value Measurement Begins with a Strong Use Case

Weak Value Framing	Stronger Value Framing	Why It Matters for AI PM
Improve efficiency	Reduce average handling time per case by 15 percent	Makes post-launch measurement concrete
Help employees work better	Reduce time spent searching policy content by 30 percent	Connects AI to a specific operating problem
Enhance customer service	Improve first-response time and reduce escalations	Supports measurable service outcomes
Automate work	Increase straight-through handling for defined low-risk cases	Clarifies the scope of value
Drive productivity	Increase resolved tickets per analyst without quality decline	Prevents vague success claims

Baselines matter more than most teams realize

An organization cannot measure improvement if it never established where performance started.

This sounds obvious, yet it is one of the most common weaknesses in AI value tracking. Teams become excited about implementation, pilot outcomes, or launch timing and only later realize they do not have a reliable pre-AI baseline. At that point, proving impact becomes difficult because no one can compare the post-launch state to a documented starting point.

The AI Project Manager should therefore ensure that baseline measures are captured early enough to matter.

Depending on the use case, these may include:

- average handling time
- cycle time
- manual effort per transaction
- routing accuracy

- rework levels
- escalation rates
- backlog volume
- cost per transaction
- throughput volume
- customer-response measures
- case-quality scores

Without baseline discipline, post-launch value claims become much easier to challenge and much harder to trust.

AI ROI is broader than labor savings

A narrow view of ROI weakens AI decision-making.

Many organizations default immediately to headcount reduction when discussing AI value. Sometimes labor productivity is a real part of the case. Often it is not the whole story. In some cases, the more realistic value lies in throughput gain, cycle-time reduction, error reduction, escalation avoidance, or supportable growth without additional hiring.

The AI Project Manager should help keep value measurement broad enough to reflect how AI actually creates impact.

AI value may come through:

- productivity gains
- faster service
- improved quality
- reduced rework
- better routing or prioritization

- reduced escalation volume
- cost avoidance
- throughput growth without added staffing
- reduced outsourced effort
- stronger compliance consistency
- better audit support
- improved knowledge access
- strategic enablement of new service capacity

This matters because some valuable AI initiatives would look weak if judged only by direct labor savings, while others look attractive in theory until hidden operating costs are included.

Good AI project management requires a full value picture.

The four most practical ways to calculate AI ROI

Many leaders still do not know what AI ROI is supposed to look like numerically. The simplest way to solve that is to recognize that there is not only one valid method. Different use cases require different lenses.

The AI Project Manager should help the organization choose an ROI approach that matches the operating model of the use case rather than forcing every AI initiative into the same template.

The four most practical approaches are:

- simple annual ROI
- payback period
- per-transaction economics
- capacity or cost-avoidance ROI

Exhibit 17B — Four Practical Ways to Calculate AI ROI

ROI Approach	Best Used When	Formula	What It Shows
Simple Annual ROI	The use case has measurable annual costs and benefits	[(Annual Benefit - Annual Cost) / Annual Cost] × 100	Overall annual return
Payback Period	Leaders want to know how fast the investment is recovered	Initial Investment / Monthly Net Benefit	Time to recover investment
Per-Transaction Economics	The AI affects high-volume workflows	(Old Cost per Transaction - New Cost per Transaction) × Annual Volume	Unit-level operational efficiency
Capacity / Cost Avoidance	AI helps absorb growth or avoid hiring/outsource spend	Avoided Cost - Annual AI Cost	Whether AI prevented future spending

---

The core formula every reader should understand

The simplest baseline formula is:

ROI (%) = [(Annual Benefit - Annual Cost) / Annual Cost] × 100

Where **Annual Benefit** may include:

- labor hours saved
- reduced rework
- lower escalation cost
- improved throughput
- avoided hiring or outsourcing
- reduced error cost
- faster cycle time with measurable business value

And **Annual Cost** may include:

- platform or model cost
- implementation and integration cost
- support cost
- governance and review effort
- training and change management
- maintenance, prompt tuning, or retraining
- content refresh and knowledge maintenance

This formula is useful because it is simple. But it should not be the only lens. AI often creates value in ways that are clearer when viewed through payback, cost-per-transaction improvement, or avoided future cost.

Practical formulas readers can actually use

The best ROI chapters are not theoretical. They show readers what to calculate.

1. Labor savings formula

Annual Labor Savings = Hours Saved per Transaction × Annual Volume × Fully Loaded Hourly Rate

Example:

- 8 minutes saved per case
- 60,000 cases per year
- fully loaded labor rate = $42/hour

Eight minutes is 0.133 hours.

Annual Labor Savings = 0.133 × 60,000 × 42 = $335,160

This is one of the most common AI ROI methods. But it should be used carefully. Time saved is not always the same as cash saved unless the organization can actually redeploy that capacity, avoid future hiring, reduce contractor cost, or increase throughput meaningfully.

---

2. Rework reduction formula

Annual Rework Savings = (Old Rework Rate - New Rework Rate) × Annual Volume × Cost per Rework Event

Example:

- rework falls from 18% to 11%
- annual volume = 40,000 items
- average cost per rework event = $14

Annual Rework Savings = (0.18 - 0.11) × 40,000 × 14 = $39,200

This works well where AI improves routing, classification, summarization quality, or decision consistency.

---

3. Escalation reduction formula

Annual Escalation Savings = Escalations Avoided × Average Cost per Escalation

Example:

- annual escalations before AI = 9,000
- annual escalations after AI = 6,300
- average incremental cost per escalation = $18

Escalations avoided = 2,700

Annual Escalation Savings = 2,700 × 18 = $48,600

This is especially useful in support, claims, case management, triage, and service workflows.

---

4. Throughput capacity formula

Value of Capacity Released = Additional Volume Handled Without Added Staff × Average Contribution or Avoided Staffing Cost

Example:

- team can now handle 12,000 more cases annually
- avoided incremental staffing cost = $95,000 per FTE
- additional volume avoids hiring 2 FTEs

Value of Capacity Released = 2 × 95,000 = $190,000

This is often more honest than pretending all time savings are immediate cash savings.

---

5. Cost avoidance formula

Annual Cost Avoidance = Future Cost That No Longer Has to Be Incurred

Example:

- organization expected to hire 3 additional analysts next year
- AI reduces that need to 1 analyst
- fully loaded cost per analyst = $88,000

Avoided hires = 2

Annual Cost Avoidance = 2 × 88,000 = $176,000

This is often one of the strongest ways to show AI value in growing operations.

Exhibit 17C — Practical Benefit Formulas for AI Use Cases

Benefit Type	Formula	Best For	AI PM Caution
Labor Savings	Hours Saved per Transaction × Volume × Hourly Rate	High-volume operational workflows	Saved time is not always cashable savings
Rework Reduction	(Old Rework Rate - New Rework Rate) × Volume × Cost per Rework Event	Classification, routing, summarization, review work	Make sure rework cost is realistic
Escalation Reduction	Escalations Avoided × Cost per Escalation	Support, service, claims, triage	Confirm incremental escalation cost is credible
Throughput Gain	Additional Volume Handled × Value per Unit or Avoided Staffing Cost	Growth without staff expansion	Prove the extra volume is truly absorbed
Cost Avoidance	Avoided Future Cost	Hiring avoidance, outsourcing reduction, overtime reduction	Avoid treating speculative savings as guaranteed

Costs must be measured honestly too

ROI is not only about benefit. It is also about cost, including costs that emerge after launch.

The AI Project Manager should help ensure that the organization does not undercount the full cost of the AI initiative. Relevant categories may include:

- model or platform cost
- implementation and integration cost
- data-preparation effort

- governance and review effort
- training and change support
- operational support
- human-review effort
- content refresh or maintenance
- prompt tuning or retraining
- incident response
- vendor dependency cost

This is especially important because some AI use cases appear highly attractive until live operating costs are included. A solution that reduces one kind of work but adds meaningful review, tuning, and support burden may have a much weaker return than the original headline suggested.

The AI Project Manager helps protect the organization from one-sided value claims.

A completed example — ROI for an AI knowledge-assist solution

The following worked example shows what a realistic AI ROI case can look like.

Exhibit 17D — Completed Example: ROI for an AI Knowledge-Assist Solution

A company launches an AI knowledge-assist tool for internal support analysts. The tool retrieves answers from internal policy and procedure content, drafts response suggestions, and reduces manual searching.

Baseline assumptions

- Annual ticket volume: **72,000**
- Average analyst search time before AI: **6.5 minutes per ticket**
- Average analyst search time after AI: **3.5 minutes per ticket**
- Time saved per ticket: **3 minutes**

- Fully loaded analyst labor cost: **$40/hour**
- Reduction in unnecessary escalations: **1,800 per year**
- Average cost per escalation: **$16**
- Repeat handling reduced by **900 tickets per year**
- Estimated cost per repeat event: **$11**

Annual benefit calculation

A. Labor savings

Three minutes = 0.05 hours

Labor Savings = 72,000 × 0.05 × 40 = $144,000

B. Escalation savings

Escalation Savings = 1,800 × 16 = $28,800

C. Rework reduction

Rework Savings = 900 × 11 = $9,900

Total Annual Benefit

Total Annual Benefit = 144,000 + 28,800 + 9,900 = $182,700

Annual cost calculation

- AI platform / model / licensing: **$54,000**
- Implementation amortized across Year 1: **$38,000**
- Integration and support effort: **$24,000**
- Content maintenance and governance effort: **$18,000**
- Training and change support: **$9,000**

Total Annual Cost

Total Annual Cost = 54,000 + 38,000 + 24,000 + 18,000 + 9,000 = $143,000

ROI calculation

ROI (%) = [(182,700 - 143,000) / 143,000] × 100

ROI = 27.8%

Payback period

Assume the upfront investment portion is **$76,000**.

Annual net benefit:

Annual Net Benefit = 182,700 - 143,000 = $39,700

Monthly net benefit:

Monthly Net Benefit = 39,700 / 12 = $3,308

Payback Period = 76,000 / 3,308 = about 23 months

Interpretation

This is a credible but not exaggerated AI ROI case.

It shows three important truths:

- the AI is delivering real value
- the return is positive, but not magical
- support, governance, and maintenance costs materially reduce the apparent headline gain

That kind of realism is exactly what many AI business cases are missing.

Not all benefits are equally cashable

One of the most important distinctions the AI Project Manager should help make is the difference between:

- **cashable savings**
- **capacity value**
- **quality or risk value**

Cashable savings are direct financial reductions the organization can clearly recognize, such as lower contractor spend or reduced outsourced service cost.

Capacity value means the team can absorb more work without additional staffing or can redirect effort to more valuable tasks. This matters, but it is not always immediately visible in the budget.

Quality or risk value may come through fewer errors, stronger consistency, better auditability, or lower compliance exposure. These benefits can be highly meaningful even when they do not look like immediate cash savings.

A mature AI value case usually includes more than one of these categories. The AI Project Manager should make sure they are not blended carelessly or double-counted.

Why projected ROI and realized ROI often differ

Many AI use cases do not miss their value targets because the model "failed." They miss because the real operating environment is more expensive, more constrained, or more behaviorally complex than expected.

Exhibit 17E — Why Projected ROI and Realized ROI Often Differ

Cause of Gap	What Happens	AI PM Question
Weak Adoption	Users underuse, bypass, or only partially trust the AI	Was adoption assumed rather than planned?
Excessive Review Burden	Human controls consume more effort than expected	Did the control model erode the projected gain?
Process Misfit	AI improves one step but disrupts the whole workflow	Was end-to-end impact tested honestly?
Hidden Operating Costs	Support, maintenance, and tuning cost more than expected	Was the cost model too narrow?
Quality Variability	AI performs inconsistently across case types	Was value overstated from pilot conditions?
Overly Broad Assumptions	Business case assumed scale or automation too early	Were assumptions validated before expansion?

Why AI ROI is often overstated

Many AI ROI claims are inflated for predictable reasons.

Common errors include:

- treating all time saved as financial savings
- ignoring human-review effort
- ignoring support, maintenance, and governance cost
- measuring one improved step while ignoring downstream rework
- projecting pilot results directly into enterprise scale
- assuming adoption will be immediate and universal
- assuming quality will remain stable without additional operating effort

The AI Project Manager should help challenge these assumptions early. A credible ROI case that survives scrutiny is more valuable than an inflated one that collapses after launch.

Different use cases need different ROI lenses

Not every AI initiative should be measured the same way.

High-volume operational AI may be best measured through handling-time reduction, cost-per-transaction improvement, escalation reduction, or throughput increase.

Knowledge-assist and copilot use cases may be better measured through search-time reduction, rework reduction, response quality, or faster resolution support.

Higher-risk decision-support AI may need stronger focus on error avoidance, compliance consistency, audit support, and targeted productivity gain.

Strategic AI capabilities may be best justified through avoided hiring, service capacity growth, or more scalable operating models rather than direct labor elimination.

The AI Project Manager should help choose the value method that best reflects the real use case. That improves both credibility and decision quality.

End-to-end impact matters more than local improvement

A common AI measurement mistake is focusing on local gains without considering end-to-end effect.

An AI tool may reduce the time required for one step while increasing downstream review effort. It may save time for senior users while confusing new users. It may improve one queue while shifting exceptions into another queue. It may reduce handling time without improving actual service quality.

The AI Project Manager should therefore encourage end-to-end impact measurement.

The right question is not simply whether the AI improved part of the workflow. The right question is whether the overall business outcome improved once the full operating process is considered.

That is the difference between local optimization and real business impact.

ROI review should happen more than once

Many organizations ask whether the AI delivered value either too early or too late.

Too early, and the service has not stabilized enough to judge fairly.

Too late, and weak performance may continue for months without challenge.

The AI Project Manager should define a practical value-review cadence, such as:

- an early stabilization review
- a more formal post-launch value review
- a broader ROI review after enough operating volume has accumulated
- periodic review for higher-value or higher-risk live services

This matters because AI value is dynamic. It may improve as users mature, or weaken as drift and maintenance cost emerge. A single snapshot rarely tells the whole story.

The AI Project Manager should help separate signal from storytelling

AI initiatives often attract narrative pressure.

Sponsors want to show progress. Executives want visible wins. Teams want recognition for innovation. Vendors want proof points. This creates subtle pressure to tell a positive story before the evidence is mature enough.

The AI Project Manager should help resist that pressure.

That does not mean being negative. It means being precise.

If the AI improved one measure but not another, that should be stated clearly.

If the value is promising but not yet fully proven, that should be stated clearly.

If the return depends on scale that has not yet occurred, that should be stated clearly.

If support cost is eroding part of the benefit, that should be stated clearly.

This is one of the most important contributions of disciplined AI project management: protecting the organization from mistaking a good narrative for a good result.

A completed interpretation example — what a steering committee should hear

Suppose an AI knowledge-assist tool shows **approximately 28 percent annual ROI on paper**. The AI Project Manager should not present only the percentage. The committee needs to understand what is driving the number, what assumptions sit underneath it, and what could cause the return to improve or decline.

In this example, the AI knowledge-assist tool supports a service organization handling approximately **45,000 support interactions per year**. Before implementation, agents spent an average of **10.0 minutes per case** searching for knowledge articles, prior tickets, policy guidance, or escalation notes. After stabilization, average search time fell to **7.1 minutes per case**, producing an estimated **2,175 hours of annual productivity capacity**.

The tool also reduced escalation volume from **18 percent to 15.5 percent**, avoiding approximately **1,125 escalations per year**. Repeat handling declined from **11 percent to 9.2 percent**, reducing duplicate or reopened work by approximately **810 cases annually**.

A simplified value view might look like this:

Value driver	**Estimated annual impact**
Agent search-time reduction	$119,625
Fewer escalations	$129,375
Reduced repeat handling	$52,650
Lower SME support and onboarding burden	$82,350
Total estimated annual benefit	**$384,000**

The financial case is positive, but not explosive. The initial implementation cost was approximately **$420,000**, with ongoing annual support, content governance, tuning, and platform administration costs of about **$160,000**. When the initial investment is annualized over three years, the tool carries an estimated annualized cost of approximately **$300,000**.

Using that view:

Annual ROI = ($384,000 benefit – $300,000 annualized cost) ÷ $300,000 = 28 percent

Payback is approximately **23 months**, based on annual net benefit after ongoing operating cost.

A stronger executive summary would sound like this:

The AI knowledge-assist tool is producing positive, measurable value in the target workflow. Average agent search time has fallen from **10.0 minutes to 7.1 minutes per case**, escalation volume has declined from **18 percent to 15.5 percent**, and repeat handling has fallen from **11 percent to 9.2 percent**. Across roughly **45,000 annual support interactions**, this translates into an estimated **$384,000 in annual business benefit**.

The return is real, but not oversized. The current annual ROI is approximately **28 percent**, with payback in about **23 months**. The business case is credible for continued operation and selective expansion, but the value depends on maintaining knowledge quality, content ownership, adoption discipline, and support capacity. If content becomes stale or agent usage drops, the ROI will weaken quickly.

The recommendation is to continue operating the capability, expand it selectively to adjacent high-volume workflows, and require quarterly value tracking before approving broader enterprise rollout.

That is how the AI PM helps leadership make a better decision. The point is not simply that the tool has a positive ROI. The point is that the ROI is **explainable, conditional, and manageable**.

What this chapter means for leaders

Leaders should leave this chapter with one clear understanding: AI value does not prove itself.

The organization must measure business impact deliberately, using baselines, explicit outcome targets, realistic cost accounting, and evidence that reflects the full workflow rather than isolated technical success. It must distinguish real business benefit from vanity metrics and separate credible value signals from optimistic storytelling.

The AI Project Manager is important here because the role helps make ROI measurable from the beginning and reviewable after launch.

Takeaway

Measuring ROI and business impact is one of the most important disciplines in AI project management. A launched AI initiative is not automatically a valuable one. Real value must be demonstrated through clear baselines, measurable outcomes, practical ROI formulas, honest cost accounting, and evidence of end-to-end improvement. The AI Project Manager helps preserve the original value logic of the project, coordinate post-launch impact review, and ensure that scale decisions are based on real return rather than excitement.

In AI, business value should not be assumed because the technology is impressive.

It should be proven because the outcomes are measurable.

Chapter 18

When to Pause, Stop, or Re-Scope an AI Project

Why this is one of the most important disciplines in AI leadership

One of the least-discussed strengths in AI project management is the ability to stop pushing the wrong thing forward.

Many organizations are comfortable talking about innovation, pilots, scale, adoption, and ROI. Far fewer are comfortable talking about pause decisions, controlled stops, or scope reduction. Yet these are some of the most valuable decisions leaders can make.

AI projects often begin with high optimism. The use case sounds strategic. The technical possibilities appear promising. Sponsors want momentum. Vendors promise acceleration. Teams become invested in making the initiative succeed. Once this happens, it becomes psychologically and politically difficult to admit that the original path may no longer be the right one.

That is exactly why discipline is needed.

The AI Project Manager should help the organization recognize that continuing is not always the most responsible option. Some projects need more time. Some need narrower scope. Some need stronger prerequisites. Some need redesign. Some need to be stopped before further effort is wasted.

This is not anti-innovation. It is one of the clearest signs of mature AI leadership.

A weak organization treats stopping as embarrassment.

A mature organization treats stopping as governance.

The AI Project Manager's role in pause, stop, and re-scope decisions

The AI Project Manager is rarely the sole decision-maker in whether an AI project should continue. Business sponsors, executive leaders, technical leads, operational owners, and governance stakeholders all play a role. But the AI Project Manager is often the person best positioned to help the enterprise see when the current path is no longer justified.

That is because the AI PM sits close enough to the delivery reality to see the evidence accumulate:

- value assumptions weakening
- readiness issues remaining unresolved
- scope staying unstable
- quality remaining inconsistent
- ownership staying unclear
- support expectations outgrowing capacity
- controls becoming heavier than the business case can support
- costs rising while benefits remain uncertain

The AI Project Manager helps turn these signals into decision-grade clarity.

That means framing the issue properly. The question is not, "How do we keep moving no matter what?" The question is, "Given what we now know, what is the most responsible next decision for value, control, and delivery realism?"

That shift is one of the most important contributions the AI PM can make.

Continuing is not always a sign of discipline

Organizations often assume that persistence is inherently virtuous. In AI delivery, persistence can be wise, but it can also become expensive denial.

A project that continues despite weak evidence is not necessarily demonstrating resilience. It may be demonstrating sunk-cost thinking.

A project that keeps broadening its scope to avoid confronting weak core performance is not demonstrating ambition. It may be avoiding reality.

A project that remains in pilot mode indefinitely is not necessarily prudent. It may be trapped between optimism and unreadiness.

The AI Project Manager should help the organization distinguish between productive persistence and unmanaged continuation.

That distinction matters because AI projects can consume significant effort even when they are not producing credible value. They can tie up scarce technical talent, stakeholder attention, governance capacity, and business patience. And if they continue too long without honest correction, they can damage confidence in future AI efforts as well.

The four responsible options

When an AI initiative is no longer progressing as expected, the answer is not always to stop entirely. In practice, there are usually four responsible options:

- pause
- stop
- re-scope
- redesign and continue under tighter conditions

The AI Project Manager should help make these options visible.

A **pause** is appropriate when the project still appears strategically worthwhile, but key conditions are not yet strong enough for responsible continuation. The organization may need time to improve data readiness, clarify ownership, resolve governance issues, or rebuild the delivery path.

A **stop** is appropriate when the use case no longer justifies continued investment in its current form. This may be because value is too weak, economics do not hold, quality remains insufficient, or the business context has changed.

A **re-scope** is appropriate when the original ambition was too broad for the evidence or support model currently available. Narrowing the use case, reducing automation scope, or focusing on lower-risk cases may preserve value while restoring realism.

A **redesign-and-continue** path is appropriate when the core problem remains worth solving, but the current design is flawed. This may involve workflow redesign, a different human-review model, a different technical approach, or a narrower operational footprint.

The AI PM role helps the organization avoid the false binary between “keep going” and “kill it.”

Exhibit 18A — The Four Main Decision Paths

Decision Path	When It Fits	Why It Can Be the Right Choice	AI PM Concern
Pause	Important conditions are not yet strong enough	Preserves the option to continue later under better conditions	Is the pause disciplined, with clear restart criteria?
Stop	The value, readiness, or economics no longer justify continuation	Prevents further waste and false momentum	Is the decision evidence-based and clearly communicated?
Re-Scope	The original scope is too broad for current reality	Protects viable value by narrowing ambition	Has the new scope been clearly redefined?
Redesign and Continue	The problem is valid but the current design is weak	Avoids abandoning a good problem because of a poor approach	Is the redesign linked to specific evidence, not vague hope?

Common reasons an AI project should be paused

Not every weak project should be stopped immediately. Some should be paused because the fundamentals may still justify future work if conditions improve.

A pause is often appropriate when:

- data readiness is materially weaker than expected
- an operational owner has not yet been secured
- governance or risk questions remain unresolved

- support capability is not yet credible
- upstream process change is still underway
- the pilot produced useful learning, but not enough evidence for progression
- key dependencies are missing but realistically fixable

In these cases, continuation may not be the problem. Premature continuation is the problem.

The AI Project Manager should help make a pause constructive rather than ambiguous. A good pause is not a vague delay. It has reasons, conditions, owners, and criteria for restart.

Common reasons an AI project should be stopped

Stopping is appropriate when the core case no longer holds.

This may happen for several reasons:

- the business value is too weak relative to cost
- performance remains inadequate despite reasonable effort
- the data conditions are too poor for the use case to be viable
- required controls make the use case economically unattractive
- the business process is too immature or unstable
- operational ownership is absent or unsustainable
- the use case was strategically interesting but operationally unnecessary
- the business environment has changed and the original problem is no longer a priority

These situations can be politically uncomfortable, especially if the project was high visibility. But allowing a weak project to continue simply because effort has already been invested is usually more damaging than stopping it honestly.

The AI Project Manager helps make this decision legible and defensible.

Re-scoping is often the smartest move

Some AI initiatives fail because the problem was wrong.

Many more struggle because the ambition was too broad.

An overly ambitious AI project may try to:

- automate too many case types too early
- operate across too many business units at once
- remove too much human review before trust is earned
- depend on data quality that does not yet exist
- support too many edge cases before the common cases are stable
- promise enterprise-wide value before the operating model is proven

In these situations, re-scoping is often the most responsible move.

The AI Project Manager should help identify where value remains credible and where the broader vision became unrealistic. A narrower use case, a smaller user population, a more limited decision scope, or a lower-risk operational boundary may preserve the initiative while restoring discipline.

Re-scoping is not retreat. It is often how a project becomes real.

Exhibit 18B — Warning Signs That the Project Should Not Simply Continue as Planned

Warning Sign	What It Often Means	AI PM Question
Pilot shows mixed value and weak adoption	The use case may not be as compelling as expected	Are we treating interest as value?
Data issues remain unresolved after repeated effort	Structural readiness may be too weak	Are we trying to build on a weak foundation?
Human-review burden is overwhelming	The control model may erase the projected benefit	Does the use case still make economic sense?
Scope keeps expanding to justify the effort	Core value may be weaker than hoped	Are we broadening because the original case is weak?
Operational owner still unclear	The AI has no credible home after launch	Who will actually live with this capability?
Costs continue rising while benefits stay uncertain	The business case may be deteriorating	Are we still funding promise instead of evidence?
"We just need a bit more time" becomes repetitive	The project may be avoiding a real decision	What exactly would additional time prove?

Sunk-cost thinking is especially dangerous in AI

AI projects are unusually vulnerable to sunk-cost bias.

The organization may have invested in data preparation, vendor setup, model testing, stakeholder workshops, pilot infrastructure, or executive visibility. Once that happens, it becomes emotionally and politically easier to continue than to reassess.

The AI Project Manager should help challenge this pattern.

Past investment is not proof that future investment is justified.

The right question is not how much has already been spent. The right question is whether the current evidence supports continued commitment from this point forward.

This is one of the places where disciplined AI project management protects the enterprise from its own momentum.

Pause and stop decisions should be based on explicit criteria

A pause or stop decision should never feel arbitrary.

The AI Project Manager should help the organization define criteria such as:

- minimum acceptable performance thresholds
- maximum tolerable support burden
- readiness conditions that must be present
- value thresholds required for further investment
- scope boundaries that must be preserved
- ownership conditions for launch or progression
- governance conditions that must be satisfied

This is important because projects often become politically charged when the decision feels subjective. Explicit criteria make the conversation more transparent and less personal. They shift the discussion from "Who wants this project?" to "What has the project actually demonstrated?"

That improves the quality of governance and the credibility of difficult decisions.

Re-scoping should be specific, not cosmetic

Sometimes organizations announce a re-scope but do not really change anything meaningful. They keep the same expectations, the same delivery pressures, and the same weak assumptions, only with different language.

That is not true re-scoping.

A real re-scope should be explicit about what is changing:

- which use cases remain in scope
- which case types are deferred
- which user groups are included or excluded
- what automation level is being reduced
- what human-review requirements are changing
- what timeline and value expectations are being reset
- what new evidence is required for future expansion

The AI Project Manager should insist on this clarity. Otherwise, re-scope decisions become cosmetic and the project remains misaligned underneath.

A pause should not become indefinite drift

One of the biggest risks in AI project governance is the indefinite pause.

A project is not stopped, but it is not actively moving. It remains nominally alive, consuming occasional attention and lingering in the portfolio without a clear future. This creates confusion, weakens reporting integrity, and can prevent more promising opportunities from receiving focus.

The AI Project Manager should make sure any pause includes:

- the reason for the pause
- the owner of the remediation work
- the specific conditions for restart
- the expected decision date or review point
- the consequences if those conditions are not met

That is how a pause remains a management action rather than a quiet burial.

Exhibit 18C — What a Good Pause Decision Looks Like

Element	Why It Matters	AI PM Focus
Clear Reason for Pause	Prevents ambiguity and rumor	Has the issue been stated honestly?
Named Owner for Remediation	Prevents drift and unclear responsibility	Who is responsible for fixing the blocker?
Restart Criteria	Creates an evidence-based path back	What must be true before work resumes?
Review Date	Prevents indefinite limbo	When will leadership reassess the decision?
Portfolio Visibility	Keeps governance honest	Is the project still being reported accurately?

Sometimes the right answer is not "stop AI," but "solve the problem differently"

An AI initiative may fail without invalidating the underlying business problem.

This is an important distinction.

The problem may still be worth solving, but perhaps not through the current AI approach. The organization may need a rules-based solution, process redesign, content improvement, workflow simplification, or a different form of automation before AI becomes useful.

The AI Project Manager should help leaders see this clearly. Stopping an AI project does not necessarily mean abandoning the business need. It may mean choosing a more appropriate path.

That protects the organization from both extremes:

- forcing AI onto the wrong problem
- abandoning a real business problem because one AI approach underperformed

---

A completed example — when re-scope is better than continuation

Consider a company developing an AI assistant for employee policy and HR support. The original ambition was broad: answer policy questions, guide employees through transactions, recommend next steps, and eventually automate some case handling.

The pilot showed mixed results. Basic policy Q&A performed well enough, but workflow guidance was inconsistent, some policy content was outdated, and the human-review burden for more sensitive cases remained high. Users liked the idea, but confidence dropped when the AI moved beyond straightforward questions.

The sponsor initially wanted to continue and "improve everything at once."

The AI Project Manager reframed the issue.

The evidence suggested that the narrow knowledge-assist use case was viable. The broader workflow-guidance and action-support ambitions were not yet mature enough. Content governance also needed strengthening before the system could be trusted in more complex scenarios.

Rather than allowing the project to continue under the original broad scope, the AI Project Manager recommended a re-scope:

- retain the AI for policy Q&A only
- defer action-guidance features
- formalize content ownership
- narrow pilot success criteria to the viable use case

- revisit broader expansion only after stronger performance evidence and content discipline were established

Leadership accepted that recommendation.

The project did not fail. It became more honest.

That is often the difference between weak AI governance and mature AI project management.

A completed example — when stopping is the right call

Now consider a separate initiative aimed at using AI to automate complex vendor-contract review across multiple regions.

The idea was strategically attractive, but the project encountered repeated barriers. Contract structures varied widely, metadata quality was poor, legal-review thresholds were high, and the human-review burden remained so heavy that the business case deteriorated. After multiple rounds of experimentation, the technical team could show pockets of promise, but not enough consistent value to justify continued investment at the proposed scope.

The sponsor argued that the project should continue because too much effort had already been invested to stop now.

The AI Project Manager organized the review differently. The evidence showed that:

- quality remained inconsistent
- data normalization work was larger than expected
- legal risk prevented meaningful automation
- projected savings were no longer credible once review cost was included
- other AI opportunities in the portfolio had stronger value and readiness

The recommendation was to stop the current initiative rather than continue consuming time on a weak and expanding case.

That was not a failure of discipline. It was discipline.

It protected the portfolio, freed capacity, and prevented the organization from calling persistence "strategy."

Stopping or narrowing a project can strengthen trust in the AI program

There is a common fear that stopping AI projects will make leadership lose confidence in the overall AI agenda.

In reality, the opposite is often true when the decision is handled well.

An organization builds trust in its AI program when people see that projects are being governed honestly. When weak projects are paused, narrowed, or stopped based on evidence, stakeholders become more likely to trust the projects that do move forward. They see that the enterprise is not blindly chasing AI, but managing it with seriousness.

The AI Project Manager helps create that trust by making difficult decisions visible, reasoned, and evidence-based.

That is one of the most underrated benefits of strong AI PM discipline.

What this chapter means for leaders

Leaders should leave this chapter with one clear understanding: one of the most valuable capabilities in AI management is knowing when not to continue.

Some AI initiatives deserve more time. Some deserve narrower scope. Some deserve redesign. Some deserve to stop. The right decision depends on value, readiness, economics, ownership, control burden, and operational reality.

The AI Project Manager is important here because the role helps surface the evidence, frame the options, and protect the organization from continuing for the wrong reasons.

Takeaway

Knowing when to pause, stop, or re-scope an AI project is one of the most important leadership disciplines in enterprise AI. Not every initiative should continue as originally planned, and persistence alone is not proof of good management. The AI Project Manager helps the organization recognize when value is weakening, readiness is insufficient, scope is too broad, or costs are outpacing benefit, and then helps structure the responsible next decision.

In AI, disciplined delivery does not mean forcing every project forward.

It means being willing to change course before false momentum becomes avoidable failure.

Part 4-NEXT WAVE

Chapter 19

Managing Generative AI Projects

Why generative AI projects require a different management posture

Generative AI projects often look deceptively easy at the start.

A team enters a few prompts, sees fluent output, and quickly imagines a long list of possible use cases: drafting responses, summarizing documents, answering questions, generating knowledge articles, assisting employees, supporting agents, or helping customers navigate processes. Because the output sounds natural and the barrier to experimentation appears low, organizations can mistake early fluency for delivery readiness.

That is a serious risk.

Generative AI projects are not difficult merely because the technology is new. They are difficult because the outputs can be persuasive without being reliable, useful without being consistent, and impressive in demonstrations while still being unsafe or weak in production. This creates a delivery challenge that is different from many traditional analytics or automation projects.

The AI Project Manager must recognize this early.

A generative AI project cannot be managed as though the main issue is simply "getting the model to work." The project must be managed around a different set of realities: hallucinations, output variability, retrieval quality, prompt sensitivity, content risk, review burden, and user trust. These realities shape the project from design through launch and into live operation.

That is why this chapter matters. Generative AI projects require adjusted expectations and stronger delivery controls.

The AI Project Manager's role in generative AI delivery

In a generative AI project, the AI Project Manager becomes even more important as the coordinator of realism.

That does not mean the AI PM becomes the prompt engineer, model architect, or content owner. But it does mean the AI PM must help the organization avoid three common mistakes:

- confusing fluent output with production readiness
- confusing pilot enthusiasm with trustworthy value
- confusing technical possibility with governable delivery

The AI Project Manager should help structure the project around the right questions:

- What kind of output quality is actually required?
- What kinds of failure are tolerable, and which are not?
- Where must the model be grounded in trusted sources?
- What review mechanism is required?
- What content risks must be controlled?
- How will users know when to trust, question, or reject the output?
- What evidence is good enough to move from experimentation to pilot to production?

This is essential because generative AI projects can move quickly in the wrong direction if they are not managed with disciplined controls.

Fluency is not reliability

One of the defining management challenges in generative AI is that output can sound confident, coherent, and useful even when it is false, unsupported, incomplete, or contextually wrong.

That changes the project-management problem.

In many traditional systems, obvious defects signal the problem. In generative AI, the output may look polished while still being unsafe for operational use. A weak summary can sound excellent. A wrong answer can appear credible. A fabricated citation can look authoritative. A customer-facing draft can feel natural while violating policy or tone expectations.

The AI Project Manager should make sure the team never treats surface fluency as proof of quality.

This means success criteria for generative AI must be more demanding than "the answer sounded good." The project needs a defined quality model, practical review criteria, and clear thresholds for what constitutes acceptable use in the specific business context.

Output variability changes how projects must be tested

Generative AI systems are not always stable in the way conventional business software is stable. The same request may produce somewhat different outputs across runs, contexts, model versions, or prompt designs. Even when the variation is not extreme, it complicates delivery.

The AI Project Manager should recognize that this means testing cannot rely on a few impressive examples.

A generative AI project needs broader evaluation across representative scenarios, edge cases, tone sensitivity, failure modes, and business-critical situations. It also needs clarity on whether variation is acceptable for the use case.

In some contexts, such as brainstorming assistance, moderate variation may be fine.

In other contexts, such as policy guidance, regulated communication, claims support, or customer advice, variation may create serious risk if the output drifts outside acceptable boundaries.

The AI PM helps make that distinction visible and operational.

Exhibit 19A — What Makes Generative AI Projects Different

Generative AI Reality	Why It Matters	AI PM Concern
Hallucinations	The model may invent facts, sources, or details	What failure types are unacceptable for this use case?
Output Variability	Outputs may differ across runs or versions	How much variation is tolerable in production?
Prompt Sensitivity	Small prompt changes can materially alter behavior	Is prompt design being controlled and versioned?
Retrieval Dependence	Grounded answers are only as good as the source set and retrieval quality	Are trusted sources defined and maintained?
Content Risk	Outputs may be misleading, harmful, off-brand, or noncompliant	What content controls and review rules are required?
Trust Illusion	Fluent output can create false user confidence	How will users be trained to use good judgment?

Hallucinations are not a side issue

For generative AI, hallucinations are not a technical footnote. They are a core delivery issue.

A hallucination is not only a strange or obvious fabrication. It may be a subtle inaccuracy, unsupported summary claim, invented citation, omitted condition, or incorrect interpretation presented with confidence. In business settings, that can be highly disruptive. It can mislead employees, confuse customers, distort analysis, or undermine trust in the AI and the broader program around it.

The AI Project Manager should help ensure that hallucination risk is addressed explicitly in the use case design.

That includes asking:

- Is the use case acceptable if the model occasionally produces unsupported content?

- Must the system be grounded in enterprise sources?
- What review is required before outputs are acted on?
- What types of hallucination are high risk for this context?
- How will hallucination frequency or severity be monitored?

The right answer will vary by use case. But what cannot vary is the need to confront the issue directly.

Retrieval quality is often the real project

Many enterprise generative AI projects are not truly standalone model projects. They are retrieval-and-grounding projects wrapped around a model.

That distinction matters.

In practice, much of the business value depends not only on the model's language ability, but on whether the system retrieves the right content, grounds the answer appropriately, avoids stale or conflicting material, and cites or reflects trusted sources correctly.

The AI Project Manager should therefore treat retrieval quality as a first-class delivery concern rather than a technical subtopic.

If the use case depends on enterprise policy, internal knowledge, product documentation, procedures, contracts, or case history, the project should ask:

- Which sources are in scope?
- Who owns them?
- How current are they?
- How are conflicting sources handled?
- How will retrieval quality be evaluated?
- How will stale content be identified and refreshed?
- What happens when the system cannot ground the answer well enough?

If these questions are weakly handled, the project may appear to be a model problem when it is actually a source-quality and retrieval-governance problem.

Prompting is not a substitute for project control

One of the reasons generative AI projects can become unstable is that teams begin relying too heavily on prompt adjustment as a substitute for disciplined delivery management.

A new problem appears, so the prompt is changed.

A user complaint emerges, so a new instruction is added.

The tone drifts, so another rule is inserted.

The output improves in one case, but weakens elsewhere.

Without control, prompt design becomes an unmanaged layer of business logic.

The AI Project Manager should help ensure that prompt changes are treated with appropriate discipline. That does not mean every wording adjustment must become a major governance event, but it does mean the project should know:

- who can change prompts
- how prompts are versioned
- how changes are tested
- what requires revalidation
- how prompt logic connects to the intended operating behavior

This is especially important in generative AI because prompts often function as behavioral control mechanisms, not just user instructions.

Guardrails must be designed as delivery controls

In generative AI, guardrails are often discussed as though they are purely technical filters. In practice, they are delivery controls.

They help define what the AI should not do, what it should redirect, when it should refuse, what tone it should maintain, what sources it may rely on, what content categories need caution, and what kinds of outputs require human review.

The AI Project Manager should make sure guardrails are treated as part of the use case design, not as an afterthought layered on at the end.

That means asking:

- What harmful or unsafe outputs are most relevant here?
- What policy, legal, brand, privacy, or reputational boundaries apply?
- What types of content should the model never generate?
- When should the system refuse or escalate?
- When is human review mandatory?
- What is the fallback path if the model cannot answer safely?

Guardrails are not there to make the project seem responsible. They are there to make the project operable.

Exhibit 19B — Core Delivery Controls for Generative AI Projects

Control Area	What It Should Cover	AI PM Focus
Approved Use Boundaries	What the GenAI system is and is not allowed to do	Is the scope clear enough to govern?
Source Governance	Which documents or knowledge sources may ground responses	Are trusted sources defined and owned?
Prompt and Instruction Control	How behavioral instructions are managed and changed	Are changes controlled and testable?
Review Mechanism	When humans must review or approve outputs	Is oversight usable in the real workflow?
Refusal and Escalation Logic	What happens when the system should not answer directly	Are fallback paths clear?
Content Safety / Policy Rules	What outputs are disallowed or constrained	Are content risks mapped to controls?
Logging and Evidence	What is captured for traceability and improvement	Can the team investigate problems later?

Review mechanisms must reflect real risk

Many generative AI projects begin with an implicit assumption that humans will "keep an eye on things." That is not enough.

The AI Project Manager should ensure that the review model is explicit and proportional to the use case.

For lower-risk internal drafting support, sampled review or user discretion may be enough.

For customer-facing communication, policy interpretation, regulated content, or high-impact recommendations, stronger review rules may be required.

The project should define:

- which outputs can be used directly
- which require human review

- which require approval before sending or acting
- what review criteria people should apply
- how exceptions and uncertain outputs are handled

This is particularly important in generative AI because the polished tone of the output can reduce human skepticism. Without explicit review expectations, users may either over trust the system or reject it altogether.

Content risk must be addressed directly

Generative AI projects create a wider range of content risks than many traditional AI systems.

The model may produce:

- false or unsupported claims
- unsafe recommendations
- policy-inconsistent language
- privacy-sensitive content
- biased or exclusionary wording
- off-brand tone
- misleading summaries
- overconfident answers to ambiguous questions

The AI Project Manager should help ensure that content risk is defined in business terms, not only technical terms.

Different functions will care about different risks. Legal may care about claims and commitments. Compliance may care about policy consistency. Marketing may care about tone and brand language. Operations may care about procedural correctness. HR may care about sensitive language. Customer teams may care about escalation and trust.

The project must convert these concerns into usable requirements, review rules, and testing scenarios.

Exhibit 19C — Common Content Risks in Generative AI Projects

Content Risk	Example	Why It Matters for AI PM
Unsupported Claim	Model states something not grounded in approved source material	Can mislead users and erode trust
Harmful Instruction	Output gives inappropriate or unsafe guidance	Can create operational or reputational risk
Policy Misstatement	AI describes internal policy incorrectly	Can drive inconsistent business behavior
Tone / Brand Failure	Output sounds careless, overly certain, or off-brand	Can damage user or customer confidence
Privacy / Sensitive Content Leakage	Output surfaces information that should not be exposed	Can create serious compliance issues
Overconfident Ambiguity	Model answers confidently when conditions are unclear	Makes human review less reliable

User trust must be built carefully

Generative AI creates a special kind of trust problem.

If the output is poor, users disengage quickly.

If the output is fluent but sometimes wrong, users may over trust it.

If leadership oversells the capability, disappointment grows when limitations appear.

If the review model is unclear, people become inconsistent in how they use the system.

The AI Project Manager should help ensure that trust-building is realistic. Users should understand:

- what the system is for
- what sources it relies on
- what it is not designed to do
- when they must verify or review
- what kinds of outputs are more or less reliable

- how to report weak answers or risky behavior

Trust in generative AI should come from controlled usefulness, not marketing language.

Generative AI projects need adjusted expectations

One of the most practical jobs of the AI Project Manager is expectation management.

Generative AI often creates pressure for speed because it appears easy to deploy at first. Leaders see fast prototypes and assume full delivery can move just as quickly. Sponsors may assume natural language means low complexity. Vendors may imply that configuration is enough. Users may expect the system to "just know" the answer.

The AI PM must counter this gently but firmly.

Generative AI delivery often requires:

- use-case narrowing
- source readiness work
- retrieval design
- prompt and instruction iteration
- policy and content-risk alignment
- review-model design
- realistic pilot boundaries
- extensive scenario testing
- stronger post-launch monitoring

That is why expectations must be adjusted. Generative AI may accelerate some forms of solution creation, but it does not remove the need for disciplined delivery.

Testing must include failure modes, not just happy paths

One of the most common weaknesses in generative AI projects is that teams test with good examples and friendly prompts while under-testing ambiguity, adversarial use, conflicting information, edge cases, and unsupported requests.

The AI Project Manager should ensure that testing includes:

- representative production scenarios
- ambiguous inputs
- edge cases
- refusal cases
- hallucination-prone prompts
- conflicting-source scenarios
- tone and policy-sensitive cases
- user misuse scenarios
- escalation and fallback behavior

This matters because a generative AI system often looks strongest in curated demonstrations and weakest where real production pressure is highest.

A completed example — managing a generative AI policy assistant

Consider an organization building a generative AI assistant to answer internal HR policy questions.

At first, the project appears straightforward. A model is connected to policy documents, and the early demonstrations are strong. Employees ask common questions about leave, benefits, and travel policy, and the responses sound helpful and natural.

A weak project approach would assume the solution is almost ready for rollout.

A stronger AI PM approach would slow the enthusiasm just enough to ask the right questions.

Are the source documents current and authoritative?

What happens when policies conflict or vary by region?

What should the system do when it cannot ground an answer clearly?

Which questions are low risk and which should be escalated to HR?

How will prompt changes be controlled?

How will unsupported claims be detected?

How will employees be trained not to treat the answer as automatically final?

The AI Project Manager would then structure the project accordingly:

- define approved policy sources
- require retrieval-grounded answers
- create refusal or escalation logic for sensitive questions
- set review rules for certain content categories
- test edge cases and conflicting-policy scenarios
- launch in a bounded pilot with visible limitations
- monitor hallucination, escalation, and user-trust signals after go-live

That is what disciplined generative AI delivery looks like. The model is not simply deployed because it sounds good. It is managed because the business must live with its outputs.

What this chapter means for leaders

Leaders should leave this chapter with one clear understanding: generative AI projects are not ordinary software rollouts with a better interface. They require adjusted expectations and stronger controls because the technology can produce fluent, useful, and risky output at the same time.

That means hallucinations, output variability, retrieval quality, prompt control, guardrails, review design, content risk, and user trust must all be managed deliberately. These are not edge concerns. They are central delivery concerns.

The AI Project Manager is important here because the role helps translate generative AI excitement into governable project structure.

Takeaway

Managing generative AI projects requires more than getting a model to produce impressive output. These projects must be governed around hallucination risk, output variability, retrieval quality, content safety, review mechanisms, and user trust. The AI Project Manager plays a critical role by structuring realistic expectations, defining stronger delivery controls, ensuring the use case is grounded in trusted sources and usable oversight, and preventing early fluency from being mistaken for production readiness.

In generative AI, the project challenge is not only what the model can say.

It is whether the organization can trust, control, and govern what it says in real work.

Chapter 20
Managing Agentic AI Projects

Why agentic AI changes the project-management challenge

Generative AI already changes how organizations think about delivery because the output can be fluent, variable, and difficult to govern. Agentic AI raises the stakes further.

An agentic AI system does not merely generate content, summarize information, or suggest an answer. It can call tools, trigger workflows, move information, take bounded actions, and influence operational outcomes directly. In some designs, it may chain multiple steps together with limited human involvement. In others, it may operate within a defined authority boundary and escalate only when it reaches uncertainty, exception conditions, or approval thresholds.

This changes the nature of the project.

Once AI begins to act, the delivery problem is no longer only about answer quality. It becomes a problem of action boundaries, approval logic, rollback capability, observability, escalation, and operational trust. A weak answer may create confusion. A weak action can create real business disruption.

That is why agentic AI projects cannot be managed as ordinary automation efforts, nor as simple extensions of generative AI projects.

The AI Project Manager must recognize that the central project question has shifted. It is no longer only "Can the system produce something useful?" It is also "Under what conditions is the system allowed to do something, how will that authority be controlled, and what happens when it does the wrong thing?"

That is the purpose of this chapter.

The AI Project Manager's role in agentic AI delivery

In agentic AI projects, the AI Project Manager becomes a coordinator of action governance.

That does not mean the AI PM personally designs every technical control or approval mechanism. But it does mean the AI PM must ensure the project answers a more demanding set of questions than traditional AI delivery usually requires.

These include:

- What actions is the AI allowed to take?
- What actions are never allowed?
- Which actions require human approval first?
- What tools can the AI call?
- Under what conditions should it stop or escalate?
- How will the organization observe what it did and why?
- How will incorrect actions be reversed or contained?
- Who owns the consequences of AI-initiated action in production?

These are not technical footnotes. They are the core delivery questions.

The AI Project Manager helps ensure that agentic AI is not treated as "automation plus intelligence" without sufficient control structure. The more the AI can do, the stronger the management discipline must be around what it is permitted to do.

Acting is not the same as recommending

A major project risk in agentic AI is that organizations underestimate the difference between recommendation and action.

In an advisory use case, the AI may suggest a route, summarize a case, or propose a response. A human still decides what happens next.

In an agentic use case, the AI may open the ticket, send the message, trigger the workflow, update the system, assign the case, retrieve the file, or initiate the transaction. Once that happens, the cost of error changes.

This is why the AI Project Manager should make sure the project clearly distinguishes among:

- AI that informs
- AI that recommends
- AI that triggers
- AI that executes within bounds
- AI that executes with later review

These distinctions matter because each one implies a different governance posture, a different testing burden, and a different level of organizational trust.

An agentic AI project is not mature simply because the underlying model is good. It is mature only when the action model is controlled.

Action boundaries must be explicit

One of the most important controls in agentic AI delivery is the action boundary.

This defines what the AI can do, what it can never do, and what it may do only under defined conditions. Without explicit boundaries, the organization is not governing the AI. It is hoping the system behaves appropriately.

The AI Project Manager should ensure that action boundaries are defined clearly enough for business leaders, technical teams, risk stakeholders, and operational owners to understand.

That usually means answering questions such as:

- What actions are in scope?
- What systems can the AI access?
- What data can it read, write, or move?
- What kinds of transactions can it initiate?
- What exceptions require immediate escalation?
- What financial, legal, operational, or customer-impact thresholds change the control model?

- What actions are permanently out of scope regardless of technical possibility?

This is essential because agentic AI often becomes dangerous not when it fails dramatically, but when its permitted scope is too loosely defined.

Exhibit 20A — Why Agentic AI Projects Are Different

Agentic AI Reality	Why It Matters	AI PM Concern
The AI can take actions, not just generate outputs	Errors can create operational consequences directly	Are action boundaries explicit and approved?
Tool calls create system reach	The AI may affect multiple systems and workflows	Which tools are allowed, and under what conditions?
Workflow chaining increases complexity	A single request may trigger multiple steps	Is end-to-end control understood?
Autonomy creates escalation questions	The system must know when not to proceed	Are stop, escalate, and approval conditions defined?
Failures may need reversal, not just correction	Wrong actions may have to be undone	Is rollback or containment possible?
Observability becomes critical	The organization must know what the AI did and why	Is traceability strong enough for production use?

Approval logic is central to safe design

The defining design question in many agentic AI projects is not whether the system can act. It is when the system may act without human approval and when it must wait.

This is where approval logic becomes essential.

The AI Project Manager should help ensure that the team defines approval logic in business terms, not only technical terms. That means understanding which factors change the acceptable control level:

- risk category
- customer impact
- monetary value
- policy sensitivity
- data sensitivity
- operational criticality
- exception conditions
- uncertainty level

For example, an AI agent may be allowed to reset routine internal access under tightly defined conditions but not approve elevated access. It may be allowed to draft and queue a standard message but not send a sensitive external communication without human approval. It may be allowed to resolve known low-risk cases but not act on ambiguous or novel ones.

The AI Project Manager helps turn these distinctions into delivery requirements rather than leaving them as vague governance aspirations.

Tool access should be governed as carefully as model behavior

In agentic AI, tool access often matters as much as model quality.

A model with modest reasoning ability but broad tool access may create more operational risk than a stronger model with narrow, well-governed action boundaries.

This is because tools give the AI reach into systems, records, workflow triggers, and business actions.

The AI Project Manager should therefore ensure that the project treats tool access as a governed delivery topic.

The project should ask:

- Which tools may the AI call?
- What can each tool do?
- Are tools read-only, advisory, or action-enabling?
- What authentication and access boundaries apply?
- Are some tools allowed only with prior approval?
- What logging is captured for each tool call?
- What fallback happens if the tool response is inconsistent or incomplete?

This is especially important because organizations sometimes focus on the model while under-governing the tool layer that actually creates operational effect.

Exhibit 20B — Core Control Questions for Agentic AI Projects

Control Question	Why It Matters	AI PM Focus
What actions can the AI take?	Defines operational authority	Is the allowed action set explicit?
What tools can it use?	Determines system reach and consequence	Are tool permissions governed?
When is approval required?	Prevents uncontrolled autonomy	Are approval thresholds clear and usable?
When must it stop or escalate?	Protects against acting under uncertainty	Are escalation rules designed into the workflow?
What can be reversed?	Limits harm from wrong action	Is rollback capability available where needed?
What is logged?	Enables traceability and incident review	Can actions be reconstructed later?
Who owns the live service?	Action-taking AI needs strong operational accountability	Is post-launch ownership clear?

Escalation must be designed, not improvised

A well-governed agentic AI system should know when not to continue.

That is why escalation design is fundamental.

The AI Project Manager should ensure that escalation is treated as part of the operating model, not merely a support fallback. The project should define:

- what kinds of uncertainty require escalation
- what exception patterns require escalation
- what confidence or rule failures trigger escalation
- who receives the escalation
- what context is passed with it
- how human reviewers can approve, reject, or redirect the next action

This matters because agentic systems often fail in the spaces between normal and abnormal behavior. If the AI can act when the workflow is standard but has no strong logic for when conditions become ambiguous, then the organization has built partial automation without safe interruption points.

The AI PM helps prevent that by making escalation pathways concrete.

Observability becomes much more important when AI can act

In ordinary software, logs often help explain what happened after a failure. In agentic AI, observability must be stronger because the organization needs to know not only whether the system ran, but what it decided, what it did, which tools it used, what information it relied on, and why it did not escalate.

The AI Project Manager should make sure the project asks for observability that is useful for governance and operations, not merely useful for engineering.

That often includes:

- input context
- decision path
- tool calls made
- approvals requested or bypassed
- outputs produced
- actions triggered
- exceptions encountered
- escalation events
- timestamps and actor traceability

Without this, post-incident review becomes weak, user trust declines, and governance bodies cannot tell whether the live service is still operating as intended.

Rollback capability is part of production readiness

One of the clearest differences between advisory AI and agentic AI is that the latter may require reversal of action.

If an AI-generated summary is wrong, it may be corrected.

If an AI-triggered action is wrong, the organization may need to undo it.

The AI Project Manager should therefore ensure that rollback or containment is discussed explicitly during delivery.

The project should ask:

- Which actions can be reversed?
- Which actions are irreversible or difficult to contain?
- What time window exists for correction?
- Who has authority to pause or contain the agent?
- What should happen if the AI takes repeated weak actions?
- Can the system be downgraded to recommendation-only mode if needed?

This is critical because some agentic use cases look attractive until leaders realize the consequences of wrong action are difficult to reverse. That recognition should happen before launch, not after the first incident.

Autonomy should be bounded and earned

A common mistake in agentic AI programs is trying to grant too much autonomy too early.

The promise of the technology encourages organizations to imagine end-to-end action quickly. But mature delivery usually requires a more gradual pattern. The AI first recommends, then perhaps triggers in low-risk cases, then acts within narrow boundaries, and only later earns broader delegated authority if evidence supports it.

The AI Project Manager should help ensure that autonomy is treated as something earned through evidence, not assumed because the system appears capable in testing.

This means asking:

- What is the lowest-risk starting point?
- What actions could be delegated first?
- What boundaries should remain fixed?
- What evidence would justify expanding autonomy?
- What conditions would require reducing autonomy again?

That is how the organization turns ambition into a governed progression rather than an unstable leap.

Exhibit 20C — A Practical Autonomy Progression for Agentic AI

Stage	AI Role	Human Role	AI PM Concern
Advisory Only	AI recommends next step	Human decides and acts	Is the recommendation quality strong enough to trust?
Assisted Action	AI prepares action for approval	Human reviews and approves	Are approval rules clear and usable?
Bounded Autonomy	AI acts in defined low-risk cases	Human handles exceptions and reviews samples	Are boundaries and escalation conditions tight enough?
Expanded Delegation	AI handles broader cases under governance controls	Human oversees, audits, and intervenes when needed	Has autonomy been earned through evidence?

Agentic AI failures are often workflow failures too

When an agentic AI project struggles, the problem is not always the model. Sometimes the deeper issue is that the workflow, authority structure, data flow, or escalation pattern was never designed for this kind of automation.

The AI Project Manager should help the organization look beyond the model when problems appear.

For example:

- a weak action may reflect poor upstream data
- repeated escalation may reflect unclear exception design
- over-approval burden may reflect bad autonomy boundaries
- operational distrust may reflect weak observability
- rollback difficulty may reflect a poor action selection strategy
- support overload may reflect that the organization launched too much autonomy too early

This is why agentic AI is a delivery-design challenge, not only a technical one.

Incident handling for agentic AI must anticipate action failure

Because agentic AI can act, post-launch incident handling must be prepared for more than wrong answers. It must be ready for wrong actions, incomplete actions, unauthorized actions, repeated action loops, and failures that move across system boundaries.

The AI Project Manager should ensure that the incident model includes:

- action-failure classification
- containment authority
- rapid downgrade or disablement options
- rollback steps where available
- notification paths for affected stakeholders
- evidence capture on action history and tool use
- post-incident review focused on boundary and control design

This matters because agentic AI incidents can quickly become operational incidents, customer incidents, compliance incidents, or reputational incidents. The response model needs to reflect that reality.

A completed example — managing an agentic AI for access-request handling

Consider an organization implementing an agentic AI capability for routine internal access requests.

The original ambition is broad: allow the AI to read the request, validate the user, check policy rules, interact with the identity-management system, provision standard access, and notify the requester. On the surface, this looks like a straightforward productivity use case.

A weak project approach would focus mainly on whether the AI can interpret the request correctly and call the provisioning tool successfully.

A stronger AI PM approach would ask the larger delivery questions.

Which requests are truly low risk?

Which access types must never be auto-approved?

What policy checks are required before action?

When is supervisor approval mandatory?

What happens when the user data is incomplete?

How will exceptions escalate?

Can incorrectly provisioned access be reversed quickly?

What audit trail is needed for each action?

The AI Project Manager would then help structure the project so autonomy is earned rather than assumed:

- start with recommendation-only mode for a defined request set
- move to approval-assisted mode for standard access requests

- allow bounded autonomous action only for tightly defined, low-risk scenarios
- require escalation for elevated privileges, conflicting data, or policy exceptions
- log every tool call and action
- define rollback steps for erroneous provisioning
- review incident and exception data before expanding scope

That is what disciplined agentic AI delivery looks like. The project is not managed around technical possibility alone. It is managed around what the organization is willing to let the AI do, under what conditions, with what controls.

Agentic AI makes operational ownership non-negotiable

An advisory AI tool can sometimes survive weak operational ownership for a period of time, even if that is not ideal.

Agentic AI cannot.

When AI can take actions, someone must clearly own:

- live-service behavior
- exception management
- action-boundary adherence
- incident response
- rollback decisions
- change approval
- ongoing trust and value review

The AI Project Manager should press hard for this clarity before launch. If operational ownership is vague, the system may still technically run, but the organization will not truly control it.

That is one of the sharpest dividing lines between experimentation and production.

What this chapter means for leaders

Leaders should leave this chapter with one central understanding: agentic AI projects are not simply more advanced generative AI projects. They create a different category of delivery responsibility because the system can act, not merely advise.

That means the project must be governed around action boundaries, tool access, approval logic, escalation design, observability, rollback capability, and operational accountability. Autonomy must be bounded and earned. Trust must be based on control, not excitement.

The AI Project Manager is important here because the role helps ensure that agentic AI is delivered as a governed operational capability rather than an uncontrolled technical experiment.

Takeaway

Managing agentic AI projects requires the organization to govern not only what the AI says, but what it is allowed to do. These projects demand explicit action boundaries, controlled tool access, clear approval logic, well-designed escalation paths, strong observability, rollback capability where needed, and mature operational ownership. The AI Project Manager plays a critical role by translating the promise of agentic AI into a delivery model that preserves accountability, safety, and business control.

In agentic AI, the real question is not whether the system can act.

It is whether the enterprise can responsibly govern the actions it allows the system to take.

Appendices

The following appendices are designed as working tools, not reference filler. Each can be used directly by sponsors, project managers, technical leads, governance bodies, and operational owners to improve decision quality across the AI project lifecycle.

Appendix A — AI Project Readiness Assessment

Use this assessment before approving discovery, feasibility, proof of concept, or pilot funding. Readiness should be judged across business clarity, data, governance, delivery capability, adoption, and measurement.

Scoring Scale

Score	Meaning
1	Not in place
2	Weak or incomplete
3	Basically defined
4	Strong
5	Fully ready

A score below **3** in any critical area should trigger corrective action before the initiative proceeds.

Section A — Problem and Use Case Readiness

Assessment Item	Score	Notes
The business problem is clearly defined.		
The problem is material enough to justify investment.		
The current-state process is understood.		

Assessment Item	Score	Notes
The target decision, task, or workflow is specific.		
Intended users and accountable owners are identified.		
The expected value is clear.		
The use case is narrow enough to test and important enough to matter.		

Section B — Strategic and Sponsorship Readiness

Assessment Item	Score	Notes
The initiative aligns to a real business priority.		
Executive sponsorship is active and visible.		
Business leadership can explain why this matters now.		
The initiative is not being pursued only because AI is fashionable.		
Competing priorities and opportunity costs have been considered.		

Section C — Data Readiness

Assessment Item	Score	Notes
Required data sources are known.		
Data access is feasible.		
Data quality is understood at a practical level.		
Data volume is sufficient for the intended approach.		
Data ownership and stewardship are identified.		
Privacy, retention, and sensitivity requirements are known.		

Assessment Item **Score Notes**

Data definitions are reasonably consistent.

Section D — Technical and Delivery Readiness

Assessment Item **Score Notes**

The technical approach is plausible.

Required tools, platforms, and environments are available.

Integration points are known.

Security expectations are understood.

The delivery team has the required skills or support.

There is a realistic path from pilot to production.

Section E — Governance and Risk Readiness

Assessment Item **Score Notes**

Risk classification has been completed or can be completed quickly.

Legal, privacy, security, and compliance stakeholders are known.

Human oversight requirements are understood.

Approval paths are known.

Incident and escalation expectations are defined.

The organization knows what evidence will be needed before scale-up.

Section F — Adoption and Measurement Readiness

Assessment Item	Score	Notes
Impacted users are identified.		
Workflow change implications are understood.		
Training and communication needs are known.		
Baseline metrics exist or can be established.		
Success measures are defined.		
A post-launch review approach exists.		

Readiness Summary

Item	Entry
Initiative Name	
Business Sponsor	
Assessment Date	
Assessor(s)	
Average Score	
Top Strengths	
Top Gaps	
Recommendation	Proceed / Proceed with Conditions / Pause / Reject

Readiness Interpretation

Average Score	Interpretation
4.0–5.0	Ready to proceed
3.0–3.9	Proceed with conditions
2.0–2.9	Address major gaps before pilot
Below 2.0	Not ready

Critical stop signals: no clear owner, no usable data path, no measurable value, no governance route, or no adoption plan.

Appendix B — AI Use Case Business Case Template

Use this template to define the expected value, cost, assumptions, risks, and success measures for an AI initiative before funding decisions are made.

1. Use Case Overview

Field	Entry
Use Case Name	
Business Unit	
Executive Sponsor	
Business Owner	
Project Manager	
Technical Lead	
Date	
Version	

2. Business Problem Statement

Question	Response
What problem are we solving?	
What is happening today?	
What is the cost, delay, quality issue, risk exposure, or service problem?	
Why does this matter now?	
What happens if nothing changes?	

3. Current-State Baseline

Baseline Measure	Current State Source / Notes
Annual or monthly volume	
Cycle time	
Cost per case / transaction	
Error or defect rate	
Rework rate	
SLA or service performance	
Customer / employee impact	

4. Proposed AI Intervention

Question	Response
What will the AI system do?	
What will humans continue to do?	
What decisions remain human-only?	
What workflow will change?	
What systems, data, or platforms are involved?	
What AI pattern is being used?	

5. Expected Value

Value Category	Baseline	Expected Improvement	Estimated Annual Impact	Confidence	Notes
Labor efficiency					
Cycle-time reduction					
Quality improvement					
Rework reduction					
Revenue uplift					
Risk reduction					
Service improvement					

6. Estimated Costs

Cost Category	One-Time Cost	Recurring Cost	Notes
Internal labor			
External services			
Data preparation			
Software / licensing			
Infrastructure / hosting			
Integration work			
Security / legal / compliance			
Training and change management			
Monitoring and support			
Contingency reserve			

7. Key Assumptions

Assumption	Validated?	Notes
Data will be accessible and usable.		
The business will adopt the new workflow.		
Model performance will meet threshold.		
Integration effort will remain manageable.		
Human review effort will not erase expected gains.		
Volume and demand assumptions are stable enough to justify investment.		

8. Key Risks

Risk	Probability	Impact	Mitigation	Owner
Poor data quality				
Weak model performance				
Privacy or regulatory issues				
Low user trust or adoption				
Hidden integration complexity				
High exception handling				
Vendor dependency				

9. Success Measures

Measure	Baseline	Target	Measurement Method	Review Frequency
Business KPI				
Operational KPI				
Quality KPI				
Adoption KPI				
Risk / control KPI				
Financial KPI				

10. Funding Recommendation

Field	Entry
Recommendation	Approve / Approve with Conditions / Defer / Reject
Funding Requested	
Funding Period	
Required Conditions	
Decision Rationale	

Appendix C — Governance Checklist for AI Projects

Use this checklist at initiation, before pilot, before production, and during major solution changes.

1. Ownership and Accountability

- Business owner assigned
- Executive sponsor assigned
- Project manager assigned
- Technical lead assigned
- Operations owner assigned
- Risk or control owner assigned
- Escalation path defined

2. Use Case and Scope Control

- Business objective documented
- Use case scope defined
- Intended users identified
- In-scope and out-of-scope decisions documented
- Human oversight requirements defined

3. Governance and Risk Review

- Risk classification completed
- Approval route identified
- Legal review completed where required
- Privacy review completed where required
- Security review completed

- Compliance obligations identified
- Vendor risk reviewed where applicable

4. Data Controls

- Data sources approved
- Data ownership confirmed
- Data quality reviewed
- Access permissions defined
- Sensitive data handling rules documented
- Retention requirements identified
- Lineage or provenance requirements considered

5. Model and Solution Controls

- Model purpose documented
- Performance criteria defined
- Testing approach defined
- Explainability requirements assessed
- Fairness or bias review completed where needed
- Monitoring requirements defined
- Rollback or fallback path defined

6. Process and Operational Controls

- Future-state workflow documented
- Human review points defined
- Exception handling process defined
- Manual override process defined

- Incident response path defined
- Change control path defined

7. Adoption and Change Controls

- Impacted roles identified
- Communication plan defined
- Training plan defined
- Adoption measures defined
- Trust and usability concerns reviewed

8. Production Controls

- Launch approval criteria defined
- Support model in place
- Logging and audit requirements in place
- Monitoring dashboards defined
- Post-launch review scheduled
- Revalidation triggers defined

9. Governance Sign-Off

Role	Name / Signature Date
Business Owner	
Executive Sponsor	
Security	
Privacy	

Role	Name / Signature Date
Legal / Compliance	
Data Owner	
Technical Lead	
Operations Owner	
Governance Chair / Approval Body	

Appendix D — Pilot-to-Production Gate Checklist

Use this stage-gate reference to support decisions to proceed, pause, stop, or re-scope.

Gate 1 — Discovery to Feasibility

Proceed only if:

- Business problem is clear
- Use case is specific
- Stakeholders are identified
- Data access appears feasible
- Initial value hypothesis is credible
- Major risks are understood
- Feasibility objectives are defined

Pause or stop if:

- The problem is vague
- No meaningful value can be identified
- Data access is unlikely
- Stakeholders are not aligned

Gate 2 — Feasibility to Proof of Concept

Proceed only if:

- Initial data review supports viability
- Technical approach is plausible
- Evaluation criteria are defined
- Scope is narrow enough to test
- Business owner agrees on thresholds

- Governance requirements are known

Pause or stop if:

- Data quality is clearly inadequate
- The concept depends on unrealistic assumptions
- The model cannot be tested credibly
- Risk outweighs likely value

Gate 3 — Proof of Concept to Pilot

Proceed only if:

- The proof of concept shows meaningful promise
- Minimum performance threshold is met
- Failure modes are understood
- Workflow implications are documented
- Live-test controls are defined
- Pilot audience and environment are selected
- Baseline and pilot measures are confirmed

Pause or stop if:

- Performance is inconsistent
- Value remains speculative
- The pilot operating model is unclear
- Human review effort makes the design impractical

Gate 4 — Pilot to Initial Production

Proceed only if:

- Pilot results show repeatable value
- User adoption is acceptable
- Risk controls worked as intended
- Exception handling is manageable
- Integration design is ready
- Support and monitoring are in place
- Production ownership is accepted

Pause or stop if:

- Pilot success required extraordinary manual effort
- Users do not trust or use the solution
- Exception rates are too high
- Production support is undefined
- Governance concerns remain unresolved

Gate 5 — Initial Production to Scale

Proceed only if:

- Value is being realized in production
- Quality is stable
- Monitoring confirms acceptable performance
- Controls remain effective at higher volume
- Process owners are ready for broader rollout
- ROI assumptions still hold
- Dependencies for scale are funded

Pause, stop, or re-scope if:

- Performance degrades at scale
- Costs rise faster than benefits
- Governance burden becomes excessive
- Business-unit or regional differences invalidate the design

Gate Decision Record

Field	Entry
Stage	
Decision	Proceed / Proceed with Conditions / Pause / Stop / Re-Scope
Evidence Reviewed	
Key Risks	
Conditions Required	
Decision Owner	
Decision Date	
Next Review Date	

Appendix E — ROI and Value Tracking Template

Use this template monthly, quarterly, or at steering reviews to track realized impact after launch.

1. Initiative Summary

Field	Entry
Initiative Name	
Business Owner	
Sponsor	
Production Launch Date	
Measurement Period	
Version Measured	

2. Baseline Versus Actual Performance

Metric	Baseline	Target	Actual	Variance	Notes
Cycle time					
Cost per case					
Manual effort hours					
Error rate					
Rework rate					
Throughput					
SLA performance					
Satisfaction score					

3. Financial Value Tracking

Value Category	Forecast Value	Realized Value	Variance	Confidence	Notes
Labor savings					
Productivity gain					
Cost avoidance					
Revenue uplift					
Loss reduction					
Risk reduction proxy					

4. Operating Cost Tracking

Cost Category	Forecast Cost	Actual Cost	Variance	Notes
Platform or usage fees				
Support labor				
Monitoring and tuning				
Human review effort				
Retraining / model updates				
Incident handling				
Vendor costs				

5. ROI Calculation

Use the following structure:

Total realized annual value
minus **total annual operating cost**
equals **net annual benefit**

Net annual benefit ÷ total investment cost = ROI %

6. Non-Financial Value Tracking

Non-Financial Outcome	Evidence Observed	Measurement Method	Confidence	Notes
Better decision consistency				
Better user experience				
Reduced burnout				
Better transparency				
Better compliance posture				

7. Risk and Control Performance

Measure	Result	Threshold	Status	Notes
Exception rate				
Escalation rate				
Override rate				
Invalid-output rate				
False positive / false negative rate				
Incident count				
Audit findings				

8. Executive Value Review

Field	Entry
Overall Status	On Track / At Risk / Under Review / Re-Scope Recommended
Top Value Delivered	
Biggest Variance from Plan	
Biggest Current Risk	
Action Requested from Leadership	

Appendix F — Executive Steering Agenda for AI Projects

Use this agenda to help leadership review AI initiatives with discipline at each major lifecycle stage.

Standard Agenda

Agenda Item	Key Questions
Opening and decision objectives	What decisions are needed today?
Review of prior actions	What was agreed previously, and what remains open?
Project status summary	What stage is the initiative in, and what has changed?
Business value update	Is the expected value still credible?
Delivery progress by stage	Is the initiative ready for the next gate?
Risk, control, and governance review	Are major risks and controls being managed appropriately?
Data, model, and integration readiness	Are core delivery dependencies on track?
Adoption and change readiness	Are users and operators ready?
Financial status and forecast	Are spend and benefits still within tolerance?
Decisions required	Proceed, pause, re-scope, or stop?
Actions and next review date	Who owns what next?

Standard Review Topics

Review Area	Typical Items
Project Status	Stage, milestones achieved, upcoming milestones, blockers, timeline shifts
Business Value	Original hypothesis, updated forecast, baseline versus actuals, evidence gathered
Delivery Readiness	Data readiness, technical readiness, integration readiness, support readiness
Governance and Risk	Risk classification, open control issues, security, privacy, legal, compliance concerns
Adoption and Operating Model	User readiness, workflow change, training progress, trust concerns, operational ownership
Financial Review	Budget spent, forecast to complete, operating cost outlook, funding request

Typical Steering Decisions

- Approve next stage
- Approve funding release
- Require additional evidence
- Pause pending remediation
- Re-scope the initiative
- Stop the initiative

Standard Steering Pack Inputs

- One-page project summary
- Stage-gate decision paper
- Updated risk summary
- KPI and value dashboard
- Financial summary
- Decision log
- Action tracker

Suggested Meeting Cadence

Lifecycle Phase	Suggested Cadence
Discovery / Feasibility	Monthly
Pilot	Biweekly or monthly depending on risk and spend
Production Rollout	Monthly
Scaled Production	Quarterly unless major changes occur

Steering Output Record

Field	Entry
Meeting Date	
Chair	
Attendees	
Decisions Made	
Conditions Attached	
Actions and Owners	
Escalations Required	
Date of Next Review	

ABOUT THE AUTHOR

Richard Syal is an AI strategy and enterprise technology leader with more than twenty years of experience helping organizations govern, deliver, and scale complex technology projects. His work spans AI strategy, ServiceNow implementation, IT governance, IT service management, agile and hybrid project delivery, business continuity, change management, and enterprise transformation.

He has led and advised large-scale programs across public and private sector environments, with a practical focus on turning technology investments into measurable business value. His expertise includes AI project governance and delivery, workflow transformation, ServiceNow platform strategy, ITIL/ITSM, portfolio management, risk management, and executive decision support.

As the author of several books on enterprise AI, including *ServiceNow AI, Done Right*, *Agent-Ready*, and *Essential Handbook to Everyday AI*, he writes for leaders, project managers, platform owners, and business executives who need practical guidance beyond hype. His work emphasizes disciplined delivery, measurable ROI, human trust, governance, and responsible scale.

In *The Enterprise AI Project Playbook*, he brings together decades of project leadership and emerging AI practice to help organizations select the right AI initiatives, manage uncertainty, prove business value, and scale AI responsibly.

Made in United States
Cleveland, OH
05 November 2026

47667144R00172